# FUTURE HERO

SCHOLASTIC

REMI BLACKWOOD

# FUTURE HERO

## MISSION TO THE SHADOW SEA

ILLUSTRATED BY ALICIA ROBINSON

SCHOLASTIC

*Special thanks to Isaac Hamilton-McKenzie and Jasmine Richards*

Published in the UK by Scholastic, 2022
1 London Bridge, London, SE1 9BA
Scholastic Ireland, 89E Lagan Road, Dublin Industrial Estate,
Glasnevin, Dublin, D11 HP5F



ISBN 978-93-5471-737-6

A CIP catalogue record for this book is available from the British
Library.



Printed in India by Sanat Printers

This reprint edition: December 2023



www.scholastic.co.uk

To my nephews Austin and Theo –
love you to Ulfrika and back! – **JR**

To my ancestors who came before me,
you inspire me to work hard and fight
every day. – **IHM**

# CHAPTER ONE

## REAL WORLD. REAL PROBLEMS.

Jarell brushed his hand over the back of his head. *It's got to be long enough now, right?* he thought. At least his hair was finally more than stubble. On his last adventure to the kingdom of Ulfrika, the magical symbol had been burnt away completely. He couldn't return until his hair was long enough to have a new symbol cut into it, but time was running out. He had to return to the ancient-future world of Ulfrika, find the remaining three Iron Animals and stop the evil sorcerer Ikala before it was too late.

Jarell couldn't wait to go back. Everything here in London felt so dull in comparison to the technicolour of Ulfrika. Especially when Jarell knew he had a quest to complete.

Jarell shoved his hands in his pockets and walked faster. He was near the alleyway, the quickest shortcut to his cousin Omari's barbershop, Fades. Perhaps today Legsy would tell him his hair was ready for a cut. Legsy ran the barbershop's VIP room, but only Jarell knew that he was really an Ancient with special powers. In Ulfrika, Legsy was known as the trickster god Olegu, and he'd been banished to Jarell's world.

Jarell turned the corner but stopped when he heard familiar laughter bouncing from the alley.

He ducked to the side and peered in to see his classmate Raheem, along with two other boys from his school, Kadon and Marc, kicking a football in the narrow lane.

"Mate! Did you see that save?" Raheem shouted.

"You're kidding?" Kadon crossed his arms. "That save was so easy my nan could of made it!"

As they squabbled, Jarell hesitated. Kadon and Marc were the first to tease him for drawing all the time in class. Was taking this shortcut worth the taunts? Just the thought of it made his legs feel weak.

*Sort it out, Jarell,* he thought. What would his new friend Kimisi, the fearless young warrior he'd met in Ulfrika, do? He smiled to himself as he pictured her: braids falling to her shoulders, chin up and spear gripped in her hand.

Kimisi would say "Baku!" and ask if a Kitikite had got his tongue. She would tell Jarell that he had words and he'd better use them. *And if anyone gives you grief, give it straight back to them with an extra serving.*

A sudden wave of courage came over Jarell. How could he ever become a strong leader – like his ancestor Kundi – if he let kids like Marc or Kadon spook him?

He strode into the alleyway before he had a chance to change his mind. Raheem, who had the ball, peered at him with annoyance.

"Hey, Jarell!" Raheem said. "We're kind of playing here!"

"I'm gonna be quick. I've got to get to Fades," Jarell replied as firmly as he could.

"Turn back, Jarell!" Marc yelled, plucking the ball from Raheem's hands and placing it on the ground ready for a spot kick.

"We're not going to tell you again!" Kadon snapped.

*You're the heir of Kundi!* Jarell reminded himself. *You found the Iron Leopard and overcame a pack of Were-hyenas! That was you!*

He ran forward, swiped the ball from Marc and kicked it towards the makeshift goal of two wheelie bins. He watched as it sailed high over the wall into a garden. A dog started barking eagerly behind the wooden fence.

"My ball!" Kadon screeched, chasing after it.

"Quick, get it before the dog does!" Marc chased after Kadon.

Eyes wide, Raheem let out a low whistle. "I didn't know you were any good at football."

Jarell rubbed the back of his neck, slightly surprised himself. "It just kind of happened."

"Well, hope your shape-up is worth it," Raheem said with a smile. "They're gonna be fuming the next time they see you."

Jarell shrugged. *I've got bigger things to worry about. Like a sorcerer with a score to settle, and three magical Iron Animals to find.*

Raheem grinned. "Don't worry. I'll try and cool them down. See you around, Jarell."

Jarell couldn't quite believe Raheem was smiling at him. He smiled back. "See you around."

He ran to the other end of the alleyway and turned the corner to Fades.

One of the customers stood at the door, shouting after someone who was already halfway down the street. "Yo, Daryl, don't forget – extra hot sauce on my curry goat!" he yelled.

Jarell slipped past him. The shop was buzzing. Jarell could just about hear an old-school reggae track over all the banter, debates and chats that filled the air.

"Cuz! Come chill! You're making my shop look messy." Omari waved Jarell over, clippers and comb in his hands. Hair trimmings decorated the floor as Jarell sat down on the long bench.

"Hey, Omari," Jarell said, then nodded to a guy called Red who was waiting patiently in the barber's chair. Red's family owned the best Caribbean restaurant in town. Sometimes Omari got free food in exchange for haircuts and he brought it around to share with Jarell and his brother, Lucas. Red's family made the *juiciest* oxtail stew.

"Shop's busy, huh?" Omari grinned. "Keep going like this and we'll need a bigger spot!" Omari pointed to the wall behind Jarell. "Say, you don't think you could sweep up a bit, eh? The broom's over there."

"Sure." Jarell grabbed the broom, glancing towards the colourful beaded curtain that led to the VIP room at the back of the shop. From the day the shop opened, everyone, even Jarell, knew that you weren't allowed to go to the VIP space unless Legsy invited you in. Most people acted like they didn't even know the room existed. Hopefully, Legsy would come out soon and see him.

"What's up, Jarell?" Omari asked. "I swear you haven't been acting yourself recently. Anything you wanna tell me?"

Jarell stopped sweeping, set down the broom and met his older cousin's eyes in the mirror. It killed him that he couldn't tell Omari about how their family were descendants of a great ruler from another world. Omari had always been there for him. He even had Jarell's drawings of Ulfrika up in silver frames on the wall for everyone to see . . . including some new ones inspired by his latest adventure. But Legsy said Jarell's family couldn't know about Ulfrika or the high-tech mirror that transported Jarell there. They couldn't risk someone else trying to cross into Ulfrika. Jarell was a Future Hero – the heir of Kundi – and the only person who stood a chance against the sorcerer Ikala.

"Nope, nothing to tell you," Jarell muttered and swallowed hard.

"OK, cuz." Omari looked thoughtful and went back to cutting Red's hair.

Jarell stared up at a drawing on the wall. No

one knew these drawings were all of real people and real places. There was the Goddess of Storms, Ayana, facing off against the evil sorcerer, Ikala. Ayana had used her magic to scatter the four powerful Iron Animals that belonged to the Staff of Kundi. If she hadn't, Ikala would have stolen them and used their power to control Ulfrika and then Jarell's own world. Jarell had found the Iron Leopard on his first trip to Ulfrika.

Three more animals remained missing: the crocodile, the snake and the eagle.

"O! My man!" someone shouted from the doorway. Jarell knew instantly it was Tai, Omari's friend. No one else shortened his cousin's name to a single letter.

Jarell noticed a package under Tai's arm, wrapped in a metallic, royal gold shade. Tai began greeting each person in Fades, asking them how they were doing and if they needed anything.

Jarell went back to sweeping. He'd managed to pile up quite a mound of coiled black hair in a corner. He glanced over at the beaded curtain, wondering what Legsy was doing.

Suddenly, something slammed against Jarell's chest. He stared down in surprise and scrambled to catch a golden package.

"I'm glad you're here, Lil Man." Tai smiled down at him. "I call that perfect timing."

"Tai? What is this?" Jarell asked. The wrapping paper was smooth and cool beneath his fingers.

"You'll see," Tai replied, sounding all mysterious.

He turned to leave.

"You're gone already?" asked Omari.

"I can't stop, brother, honestly. Gotta go, everyone!" Tai called out. A chorus of warm goodbyes followed him.

Jarell caught Omari's eyes and his cousin winked at him. "This is for me?" Jarell questioned.

"It's a little something to cheer you up," said Omari.

"But—" Jarell began.

"Just open it!" Omari exclaimed.

# CHAPTER TWO

## ART OF THE FIGHT

Jarell ripped the package open and gasped at the sketchbook of creamy paper and the wooden box of Aquarell pencils. They were the ones his favourite illustrator, Arter, used. Lightfast. Water-soluble. The Ferrari of pencils. *Omari must have dropped some serious cash on them . . .*

"Is that a smile I see?" Omari raised an eyebrow.

"Omari . . ." Jarell began. "This is too much . . ." He hugged his cousin. "I don't know what to say."

Omari smiled. "Don't say anything. Just get drawing."

Jarell's heart was pounding as he sat down on the bench. He opened up the sketchbook. Jarell had been drawing Ulfrika his whole life, but had not known it was real until a few weeks ago. *What will I draw this time?* he wondered.

As he looked at the blank paper, he felt the Ulfrikan heat on his skin. He could smell the rich earth of his ancestors' homeland. The pencil in his hand moved furiously across the paper... Something was taking shape.

*Huh?* Jarell thought, staring at his drawing. *What is this thing? Why would I draw this?*

It was an ugly-looking creature. It had a thick, round body like a hippo, but with short and stout

flipper-like arms. It had a narrow head and deep, jet-black eyes.

Jarell ripped the picture out and flipped to another blank page. He started again, and again. But the drawings of the weird-looking creature kept flowing from his pencil.

Jarell threw the sketchbook down by his side and sighed deeply. Nothing seemed to be going right at all.

"How you finding the pencils, cuz?" Omari called over.

Jarell looked up. How could he explain that he seemed able to only draw one thing, without disappointing his cousin and sounding ungrateful?

"They're sick," Jarell answered. "It's just . . ."

Jarell considered explaining, but thought better of it. "I guess I'm just having an off day – inspiration-wise."

Omari kept cutting. "Artist's block, huh?" He lowered his voice. "Sometimes I find a change of environment helps when you're feeling stuck. Why don't you go see what Legsy's doing in the back? Tell him I sent you! Besides, I know he'd like to see you."

Not needing to be asked twice, Jarell leapt up and swiftly tucked the sketchbook and pencils under his arm. He slipped through the curtain of colourful beads into the VIP room. The noise of the barbershop was instantly replaced by the sound of drums. Soft lighting pulsed in time to the beat.

Legsy was stretched out across one of his super slick barber's chairs. It was sometimes hard to imagine him as an immortal superbeing exiled from another world. He just looked like an old guy chilling in a barbershop.

"Mbata, Jarell." Legsy raised a hand in greeting, but he didn't look away from his mirror. Inside the dark, ancient-looking wooden frame could have been the world's most high-definition TV, but Jarell knew better. The mirror's blend of ultra-high tech and Legsy's own magic could transport a person to Ulfrika.

"Watch this," Legsy said, pointing to the mirror's surface where two warriors circled each other inside a ring made of red clay. One wore a robe of vivid yolk-yellow and the other was dressed in azure-blue. Around their ankles and wrists, narrow metal bracelets sparkled with power.

As they began to spar, the beating drums quickened. Their bodies moved with such sharp and deadly speed that Jarell wondered if the scene was on fast-forward.

"This is amazing!" Jarell exclaimed. He paused. "What's going on, exactly?"

"You are watching art," Legsy answered, his accent a mix of so many places. "We call it Ingalo. A popular combat sporting event in Ulfrika. We learn the art of Ingalo from birth, and for a lot of Ulfrikans, competing is a coming-of-age moment.

You walk into the arena as a child, and leave prepared for any challenge that may come."

Jarell's eyes widened. *How different would my life be if I'd been taught Ingalo at school?* He'd have nothing to fear from Kadon or Marc, and it would definitely help him stop Ikala, the evil sorcerer.

"But, of course, there is nothing like watching a battle in person." Legsy's voice was sad.

Jarell bit his lip. He knew it was a sore point, but perhaps this time Legsy would tell him. "Why *did* you get banished from Ulfrika, Legsy?"

The Ancient raised himself slowly from the barber's chair and pressed the edge of the mirror's frame. The Ingalo match vanished, and the mirror became a silver surface once again. "I made a mistake," he said finally. "Not everyone could forgive me. I'm safer here."

"But what *actually* happened?" Jarell pressed. "It must have been serious if you can never go back, right? Kimisi said—"

"Some stories have a time and place," Legsy interrupted. "I will tell you when the moment is right. But that time is not now."

Jarell nodded. He didn't like hearing the pain in Legsy's voice.

"Hey, how about I teach you some Ingalo?" Legsy suggested. "Find out what the descendant of Kundi is capable of."

Jarell lifted his chin. He was more than ready. *Right?*

"Let's go," Jarell said.

They started with basic fighting stances, but Jarell's legs quickly ached as Legsy kept correcting his position. Jarell needed to keep his body low and his feet wide apart. This made it easier to lunge

into attack or fall back.

"Ingalo is about timing and precision," Legsy explained. "It is about being patient and finding the perfect moment to strike." The Ancient made a steeple of his fingers. "Imagine us being the tide," Legsy explained. "Our bodies move like the waves of the ocean but with the power to change an entire coastline at any moment."

Soon, many of the movements felt like second nature to Jarell. He slid in different directions with ease, swept forward and caught Legsy off balance with a swiping kick. Legsy didn't fall to the ground, though. He was far too nimble and agile. He flipped over backwards, landing perfectly upright like a cat.

"Hah! The heir of Kundi has potential." Legsy clapped loudly. "You're raw, of course, but strong and swift like the Iron Leopard. Impressive."

Catching his breath, Jarell beamed with pride. He gave Legsy the customary bow of respect that he had been taught.

"I know you said I must be patient, but does this mean I'm ready to go back to Ulfrika?" Jarell asked. "I'll be a better warrior now. Plus my hair has grown: look!" As Jarell bent to show Legsy his head, he felt something fall from his pocket. It was a page, ripped out from his sketchbook.

Legsy stooped down and stared at the strange creatures scribbled on the paper.

"Now, now, now. What do we have here?"

# CHAPTER THREE

## TIME WAITS FOR NO ONE

"They're funny-looking, I know." Jarell's cheeks grew hot with embarrassment. "I can draw better than that, though."

"Why didn't you show me these before?" Legsy said, snatching the paper up.

"I didn't think they were anything to show. They're not even Ulfrikan . . . *are they?*"

"They're Manatees." The trickster god pronounced it with a loud click of the tongue. "Manatees, from the Koffi River. *Only* from the Koffi River. They're Ulfrikan indeed, Jarell."

Jarell's brow wrinkled. *Even if the Manatees are Ulfrikan, why am I drawing them? How could a Manatee possibly help me? It isn't even one of the four Iron Animals on the Staff of Kundi.*

Muttering something under his breath, Legsy tapped the paper against the mirror. Its silver surface rippled like water, then their reflections disappeared to reveal dense jungle. The view panned over to a wide river, just like in a nature documentary. Jarell could see the pictures he'd been drawing come to life. Two large Manatees nosed through the plants in the muddy water, thrashing with some speed. Their dark eyes flashed with fear.

"I don't know if this is the future or the past, but something has disturbed them," Legsy whispered slowly. "Your drawings, Jarell... They're a sign."

"A sign of what?" Jarell stared into the mirror. "Has Ikala caused this? Is he trying to hurt them?"

Legsy shook his head. "That is not it."

"I don't get it," Jarell said. "How are these creatures telling us anything?"

"My boy, you have much to learn. We will not learn until we know. You're needed in Ulfrika, Jarell. The Manatees will help you. Trust me." Legsy circled around Jarell. "Your hair is not as long as I would have hoped for, but it will have to do. The symbol must be placed on the back of your head. Come. Time waits for no one – not even the heir of Kundi."

"So I can return?" Jarell asked eagerly.

"You can return," Legsy said, "and be the Future Hero I need you to be. You must find the next Iron Animal of the Staff of Kundi. They are in a new order because you are a new Future Hero. You must seek the Iron Crocodile next. The Manatees are a clue that you will be heading for the water. This is where the Iron Crocodile will be."

Jarell puffed out his chest and nodded as confidently as he could. He thought of Ayana's battle with Ikala and how the evil sorcerer had almost killed her. Jarell remembered Ikala's wicked smile. Its sharpness. Like a sword that would cut away all joy in the land of Ulfrika. It was Jarell's mission to stop him.

"I'm ready," Jarell said, exhaling.

"Good." Legsy slid the barber's chair out from under the counter.

Jarell wiped his sweaty hands on his jeans and sat down.

Legsy cleaned his clippers with a brush. "Pick a

symbol," Legsy said softly. "It should be your choice."

Jarell gulped and stared at the symbols carved into the dark wood of Legsy's mirror. Every time he looked at it they seemed to change, or perhaps he just noticed different ones. He could see lizards, palm-like trees and beehives.

The last time he had gone to Ulfrika, Legsy had chosen the symbol of leadership for him – four concentric ovals, one inside the other. *Which one should I choose?* He reached out and traced his fingers across one of the carvings. A sense of peace came over him. A salty, warm breeze played across his skin, and in the distance he could hear the crashing of waves.

"It's this one," Jarell said, fingers resting on a curved line. "The wave."

Legsy nodded. "A symbol of determination. Of an unstoppable force. Of knowing when to strike, and when to fall back. Yes, the wave is a good choice."

The clippers hummed to life as the old god's face narrowed in concentration. Jarell had been longing for this moment for weeks, but now it had arrived he felt doubts.

*What if I've forgotten how to be the hero that Legsy, Ayana and Kimisi say I am? What if I fail to find the Iron Crocodile for the Staff of Kundi? What if giving me this quest has all been a big mistake?*

"Finished!" Legsy announced. He lifted a hand mirror and showed Jarell the zigzag pattern in his hair.

Legsy set the hand mirror down and spun Jarell around in the chair. He stared at him intently. "Remember, Jarell, you must return before the symbol in your hair starts to burn. If you don't, you risk being trapped in Ulfrika for ever."

*Would that be so bad?* Jarell's thoughts whispered. Ulfrika was much more exciting than South London. But then Jarell thought of his parents. He hated the idea of not seeing them again. He'd even miss his brother.

"I understand."

Jarell's skin tingled as Legsy chanted softly underneath his breath. The wavy lines in the ebony frame glimmered like moonlight on a dark sea.

In the mirror, Jarell's clothes seemed to be morphing. His plain T-shirt was gone, replaced with a high tech, black collarless suit. The crimson Ulfrikan designs that ran over his shoulders changed to match the shapes in his hair. Jarell reached out for the rippling surface of the mirror. It crackled with power as he touched it. Liquid light flowed over his hands and up across his body. Suddenly, the pattern in his hair burned hot and painful. Jarell cried out, but already the VIP room of the barbershop had vanished.

*Thump!*

Jarell hit the ground with a roll and almost instantly started sliding down a slope. He scrambled to stop himself falling as he spotted a deep-looking river below. Grabbing a twisted tree root, Jarell held it tightly and pulled himself up. He crouched a little to keep his balance, and it reminded him of his stance during his introduction to Ingalo with Legsy.

He looked up at the waterfall-blue of the sky and the intense greens of the jungle around him. He'd love to be drawing this right now with his new pencils.

*Welcome home,* the voice of his ancestor whispered to him. The words vibrated through him, from the soles of his feet to the top of his head.

Jarell carefully stood up straight. The fresh smell of rainwater and dirt was so strong he could almost taste it.

*What now?* he wondered. *Where do I go from here?*

Something caught his eye in the dark water below, stirring up the thick silt. It was a large shape, followed by another. Were they Manatees?

Jarell made his way to the bank to get a better look. But the closer he got, the harder it was to see the creatures. He balanced on the edge of the riverbank so that he could see more clearly.

Jarell's foot slipped.

*"Aah!"*

He plunged into the murky water, and the coldness of the river made him gasp. He could feel that something was close. He tried to swim back to the bank but found that the water only came up to his waist. He tried to wade instead but felt something curl around his left leg and hold on tightly.

He was trapped.

*Man, I could really use the Staff of Kundi,* he thought to himself. The fire from the Iron Leopard would scare off whatever had him in its grasp – whatever was trying to drag him down.

Body tensed, Jarell tried his best to remember an Ingalo move that Legsy had taught him. Using all his might, he struck his right foot down! He was instantly released, and he swiftly splashed through the muddy river towards the bank. As he did so, he heard something emerging from the water.

He turned around slowly. Facing Jarell was a figure, a little taller than him, wearing sleek black waterproofed armour decorated with glowing gold and red patterns from head to toe. Their face was hidden by a reflective, mirror-like helmet. It reminded Jarell of the helmets in Lucas's computer games.

"Trust it to be you," a familiar voice said from the behind the helmet.

# CHAPTER FOUR

## DANGER! DANGER!

"Kimisi?" Jarell murmured.

The figure in black pressed a finger to their forehead. The visor became clear and then, piece by piece, the helmet folded away, revealing a girl with long, canerowed hair and three golden dots painted under her left eye.

"It *is* you!" Jarell exclaimed.

Kimisi narrowed her eyes in annoyance. "Why are you smiling at me like that, Jarell?" she snarled. "You've ruined days of hard work. I was gaining their trust. Now look! They're swimming away." She pointed to the water where the dark shapes were quickly fleeing. She rubbed her arm. "And you *kicked* me! You'd think you had hooves for feet."

Jarell frowned, unsure how the blame could be placed on him. "You had hold of my leg. I thought you were some kind of terrifying water . . . goblin."

"Water goblin?" Kimisi repeated. "Are you actually calling me a water goblin?"

"No, of course not," Jarell held up his hands.

"What is a goblin anyway?" Kimisi asked.

Jarell shook his head. "It doesn't matter. I didn't hurt you, did I?"

Kimisi put her hands on her hips. "As if. The only thing you damaged is the mission to find the

Iron Crocodile. The seeing bowl told me to come here and speak with the—"

"The Manatees," Jarell blurted out. "I've been drawing them."

Kimisi raised an eyebrow.

For a moment, Jarell wondered if she might just be a little impressed with him.

"Yes, the Manatees," Kimisi went on. "I've been everywhere trying to track those creatures down and find out what they know. Ancients help me... We're running out of time." She kicked out at the water in frustration. "The whole of Ulfrika has been alive with chatter over Ikala's return. Some have even chosen to stand *with* him."

"How could *anyone* support Ikala?" Jarell was outraged. If he knew Ikala was no good for Ulfrika as an outsider, why couldn't everyone else see that?

"Some people prefer their leaders to be ferocious rather than fai— Ouch!" Kimisi gave a yelp and looked down.

Jarell followed her gaze and saw a trail of deathly pale ants trooping up Kimisi's leg. Kimisi swiftly brushed them off. "Death Ants. They only appear when evil is close by. Come, I think Ikala might be in the area. It would be foolhardy to stand still."

"But what about the Manatees?!" Jarell said, louder than he'd planned. A few frightened birds fled from the trees. "I've been drawing them non-stop. They can help us find the Iron Crocodile!"

"*Haba!*" Kimisi exclaimed. "Why do you think I am here? It took days for the Manatees to even speak with me."

"They speak too?" Jarell remembered his

friend Chinell, the Painted Wolf who had helped him last time he was in Ulfrika. "Does every Ulfrikan animal talk?"

Kimisi tutted, tapping her intricate headpiece. Bright lights danced across it, and it whirred away like a gaming console booting up for action. "They don't speak our language. This translator helps us understand each other."

"Well, if I can borrow it, I can apologize for scaring them. Then your hard work won't be wasted."

Kimisi stepped back, tutting again. "My hard work will be wasted by you wearing that outfit." She looked him up and down. "How do you think you'll breathe underwater, let alone speak with the Manatees? Luckily, I've been anticipating your return. Follow me."

Jarell grinned, realizing that he'd really missed

Kimisi's special way with words. He followed her on to the bank and along the river's edge to a shallow, flatter bank of grass, trimmed and as soft as a cloud. Jarell looked over his shoulder. Anything could be lurking in that rough field of green. *Even Ikala . . .*

Kimisi made a swiping movement in the air and, like magic, a sleek metallic chest appeared in front of her. She opened it, fishing out two identical outfits. "Put this on."

Jarell pulled it on over his clothes. *Kimisi's*

*having a laugh*, he thought. The wetsuit looked like he could fit two of himself in it. The ends hung over his limbs like Lucas's old hand-me-downs from school. "Do you have anything in a smaller size?" he asked.

Kimisi chuckled, pointing at a button on Jarell's chest. "Press it."

Jarell did, and there was a sharp zipping sound. The wetsuit rippled over his skin like a living thing and then shrunk to a perfect fit. "Wow," he said, flexing an arm as the material gripped his body.

"Take these too." Kimisi handed him two items: a power cuff that melded to his wrist and almost became invisible, and a headpiece. "This headpiece has an oxy-neuro mesh. It'll allow us to breathe and speak with each other underwater."

"Cool, like a walkie-talkie!" The intricate headpiece felt lighter than Jarell imagined, but it was still sturdy. He slid the edge of the mesh against his hairline and the headpiece vibrated as it moulded to his skin.

Jarell tapped his forehead like Kimisi had done. A faint hum of static surrounded him and a see-through visor appeared over his face, like the most massive wraparound glasses ever. "Do you think these Manatees know where to find the Iron Crocodile?"

Kimisi shrugged. "Crocodiles are masters of concealing themselves – I have no doubt the Iron Crocodile is well-hidden. At least Ikala doesn't have it, or any of the other Iron Animals that belong to the Staff of Kundi. If that was the case, he'd have drained their magic already and half of Ulfrika would be in flames by now." Shadows of worry were all over Kimisi's face. "Ikala will only get bolder and more vicious over time. This is why we must reassemble the Staff of Kundi and keep it from him."

*The Staff of Kundi.* Now that Jarell was in Ulfrika again, his hand ached to hold the staff that had once belonged to his ancestor. He ached to feel the sense of belonging and connection to the land that the staff brought to him. That feeling of homecoming he had never known that he missed.

Jarell could feel power radiating from the chest. He edged forward. It was like he was being pulled by a magnet. Reaching into the chest, the Staff of Kundi materialized in his hands.

"Finally," Jarell whispered. He pulled it close and looked down at the Iron Leopard on the tip of the staff. *Just three more to find . . .*

"Yes, finally," Kimisi said. "You've been gone

for weeks. Now, let's move—"

"Hold on," Jarell called. "Why don't I just use the staff to unearth the Iron Crocodile? The staff is the Iron Animals' home after all, and when we were looking for the Iron Leopard the staff helped lead us in the right direction."

Kimisi crossed her arms. "Go on, then."

The sun shimmered against Jarell's skin and the wind blew across his face. He gave a little cough. He deepened his voice so that he sounded especially heroic. "Return the Iron Crocodile to this place you call home . . . um . . . now, please."

Nothing happened.

"Not so easy, is it?" Kimisi said with a wry smile. "I told you, the crocodile is a master of concealment. Also, Ayana's storm magic hid the animals well. Our mission to find it and the other animals won't be an easy one."

Jarell nodded but ground his heel into the earth in frustration. *The answers are already yours, Jarell,* whispered the voice of his ancestor, Kundi. *You must seek what is already there . . .*

"Come!" interrupted Kimisi, hurrying to the riverbank. "Let us go find those Manatees!"

Kimisi activated her visor and dived into the water. As the staff shrank down, Jarell attached it to his belt loop. He then lowered himself until he was completely submerged.

"I can't see a thing!" Jarell cried. The water, thick and silty, turned everything in front of him black. Suddenly, his headpiece started to vibrate – as if it was adjusting to his environment. A red light cut a path ahead of him, making the water look completely clear.

Kimisi appeared, treading water in front of him.

Jarell could see her face behind the visor and could hear her whistling. *Strange time to be whistling,* Jarell thought.

"Why haven't you pressed the button?" Kimisi asked, pointing to his wrist.

"Because I didn't know I was supposed to."

"Baku! Sometimes I forget how little you know about our world. Press the green button on your wrist. Then you'll be able to understand."

"Understand what?" Jarell pressed the button and Kimisi's whistles morphed into words.

"Come to us," Kimisi whistled. "There is no enemy of yours near."

Jarell could see dark shapes edging closer. He heard them ask each other: *Is it true? Is it true?*

"We are friends," Kimisi called. "Do not fear."

One of the dark shapes approached, its

round body and flipper-like arms moving through the water. Seeing the Manatee up close, Jarell felt bad that he had ever thought them ugly. They were just unique. Even a bit human-looking, at certain angles. The Manatee stared at Jarell with uncertainty behind its blinking jet-black eyes.

"Trust!" it called out. Suddenly many more Manatees surrounded them.

Kimisi grinned at Jarell. "How do you do that? I've been here for days. Animals just love you!"

Jarell shrugged. "What can I say? I'm a nice kid."

"Hi hi hi," the Manatees chimed. Big ones, small ones, babies, and the rest of their friends surrounded Jarell and Kimisi. "Hi hi hi, fallen-from-the-skies ones!"

Even with few words, Jarell could tell the

Manatees' pleasant nature. Their smiles were bright and happy. Young Manatees circled and bounced all around them, and a baby no bigger than a puppy nuzzled at his leg.

"Friends," Kimisi called, "can you guide us to what we seek? We need help urgently."

The Manatees stopped their song and circled through the water, humming until their words became clear.

"The mother is strong, and the ocean is wide. It is in plain sight, yet a curse still hides." Several of the Manatees repeated the phrase again and again, circling Jarell and Kimisi so quickly that Jarell began to feel dizzy.

Two other Manatees broke away from the swirling bodies and began combing the riverbed with their flippers.

"What are those two doing?" Jarell asked. "Are

they looking for food?"

"Just wait," Kimisi said calmly. "I think they have a plan."

With powerful strokes, the Manatees returned with long, green waterweeds dangling from their mouths at either side. One of the Manatees nuzzled Jarell's arm and he understood. He took up both ends so that the weeds became reins, floating above the beast gently. The Manatees planned on taking them somewhere.

"How *fast* are Manatees, exactly?" Jarell asked, trying not to sound concerned. He knew that dolphins were pretty fast, for example. He'd seen videos of them racing through water.

"Hard to say," Kimisi answered, holding on tighter to her own Manatee. "When they need to, Manatees can be as fast as any ocean creature ...

but only if they choose to be."

Jarell raised his eyebrows. "Well, I think we should hold on ti—" He broke off as they were tugged down the river.

After a few seconds, Jarell realized he needn't have worried. Despite their enthusiasm, the Manatees weren't exactly in a hurry. The herd of Manatees followed them and sang and grazed and chatted

amongst themselves as they meandered through the water.

"See what I mean?" Kimisi gave a sigh. "Manatees are always on their own time, but we must trust in them."

Suddenly, the Manatee that was pulling Jarell along stopped. The herd shivered, twisting their round bodies in a panic. *"DANGER! TOO MUCH DANGER!"*

# CHAPTER FIVE

## A Call to Power

"What's wrong?!" Jarell called out, gripping the reins tightly. "Where's the danger? Tell us, we can help!"

But the Manatees didn't seem to hear him. They crashed against each other with such force that Jarell wondered if he and Kimisi would get crushed.

*"Danger! Too much danger! Danger!"*

"It's no use, we can't control them!" Jarell cried. "We have to let go!"

He and Kimisi released the reins and the Manatees scattered. "Farewell," the Manatees cried. "What you seek is no longer meek. Soon the truth you will meet."

At that Jarell paused. Even Kimisi looked a bit shaken. "That doesn't sound too promising," he said.

Kimisi raised an eyebrow from behind her visor. "No . . . it doesn't."

The two of them swam onwards, but the water churned around them and kept pushing them back. Rocks and weeds spun all around them, and small creatures in shells were flung from their homes.

*Something bad is causing this,* Jarell thought, *but we have to keep going.* Jarell looked out to the distance, but all he could see was water and silt. "Onwards," he said as confidently as he could.

Kimisi kissed her teeth. "These waters are large and wide and hold more than you can imagine, heir of Kundi. It is not safe like your world."

"Hey!" Jarell exclaimed. "We have our own waters too, thank you very much. And they're just as large and wide as Ulfrika's. Like the Thames."

"I'm sorry," Kimisi said. "Onwards it is. You can tell me all about the wild waters of the Thames and what lurks there later."

Jarell thought about the shopping trolley he'd seen once, floating in the water near where he lived. *Yup, there are definitely things lurking in the grey waters of the Thames.*

"You're right as well, Kimisi. We shouldn't just head into danger without a plan," agreed Jarell. "We'll get a better view from above."

They kicked up until they broke the surface and now found themselves at the mouth of a glistening lake. But the lake's entrance was blocked by a series of floating platforms. To Jarell they looked like lily pads.

On each of the lily pads stood a warrior in red-and-white armour holding high-tech tridents. The women stood with their backs

to Jarell in a tight circle. They stared down patiently at the churning water below them.

As one, the warriors fired their tridents, blasting coloured pulses into the water. Jarell couldn't see what they were shooting at, but he could feel the vibration of a roar of rage from a creature just out of sight beneath the water. Even at this distance, the cries sliced through his mind.

The warriors continued to fire pulses into the water. The creature screeched again, and its thrashing turned the water into a thick, foamy mass of spray.

"We can't let them kill that poor creature!" Jarell whispered to Kimisi. He glided towards the platforms where the warriors stood, facing away from him. "We have to help it!"

"Hold on," Kimisi urged in a low voice. "This tale might not be as simple as it seems."

Jarell whirled to face her. "What do you mean?"

"I'm just saying we don't know the full story yet." Kimisi put a hand on his arm. "We should wait and see."

Wails pierced the air again. It made Jarell's stomach squirm. This poor creature didn't stand a chance against so many well-armed warriors. Jarell thought back to school and having Marc and Kadon gang up on him in the playground.

Wasn't it his duty to protect the helpless? *What would Kundi do?*

"Enough!" Jarell exclaimed.

He reached for his staff, which was hooked at his waist. He gripped the iron staff tightly as it extended. "I summon the power of the Iron Leopard!"

Suddenly, yellow flame surrounded him, sparking from his fingers all the way down to his toes. The leopard roared in Jarell's mind as the staff's power surged through him, and he saw the leopard's eyes flash red. *I need to move. Fast.*

Jarell's body started to vibrate, and then he was surging forwards. His feet kicked faster and faster, until he found himself sprinting across the water and towards two lily pad platforms.

Now he needed a plan. Perhaps he could draw away the warriors' attention, give the poor creature a chance to escape.

He sprang into the air, landing on one of the empty lily pads near a warrior. "Hey!" he yelled as loudly as he could. "Leave that creature alone!"

No luck. Drowned out by the shooting pulses, the warrior could not hear Jarell's cries for them to stop. Her focus was on the creature in the water.

Jarell looked around. He could not see Kimisi, but he did spot another lily pad that floated near the churned-up water where the creature thrashed. It was where the warriors where shooting. *If I can get on that lily pad, they'll have to stop shooting. Right?*

He moved back as far as he could to give himself a run up, and then leapt through the air.

"I said: stop!" he cried as he landed, perfectly balanced in the centre of the lily pad. Jarell rode it like a surfboard on the churning waves.

One by one, the warriors lowered their tridents, halting fire.

"This is official business," one of the warriors called out sternly. "Remove yourself, stranger, before you get hurt." Their tridents whined as they charged up once again.

"I can't let you hurt whatever is below the water," Jarell cried.

"Hurt?" The warrior who'd spoken to him looked aghast. "We only seek to protect."

The waves beneath Jarell suddenly stilled.

"It comes," whispered another warrior.

Now Jarell could see their faces properly, what he assumed was cruelty looked more like fear. *Perhaps Kimisi was right and there is more to this story.* He searched around for his friend, hoping she was safe.

A warrior let out a cry of alarm as the water surrounding her high-tech lily pad began to boil furiously.

"Jump, Shemina!" another warrior cried, just as a gigantic horn burst through the middle of the disc and shredded it in a blaze of sparks. The horn

missed Shemina, but it kept rising from below, growing taller and thicker with sharp barbs all the way along.

Shemina jumped and landed safely on the next lily pad as the rest of the creature emerged from the water for a moment. Despite its yellow and green scales and massive horn, it looked like a killer whale. It sank back beneath the waves.

"You look like a Kitikite has got your tongue," Kimisi said as she hauled herself up on to Jarell's lily pad. "Having second thoughts about saving this creature?"

"I don't know," Jarell said truthfully. "What is that thing?"

"It's a Utelif."

"A what?"

"A Utelif is one of Ulfrika's great whales," Kimisi explained, then frowned. "They are majestic creatures but are never found in freshwater because it is poisonous to them. Utelifs find home in saltwater, like the Shadow Sea. Perhaps the warriors were trying to guide it there?"

"Well, it wasn't working," Jarell replied. "We need to help them calm the creature down, not keep freaking it out."

Kimisi nodded. "I agree. If we get close enough I could sing to it with griot magic. I can try that at least."

They dived underwater, and Jarell saw more warriors beneath the lily pads. These wore darker shades of high-tech clothing with bright orange and silver symbols woven into the material. Fins sprouted from their arms and legs.

"No way," Jarell gasped. *Are they mermaids?*

The warriors were trying to corral the Utelif into a net using pulses from their wrist-mounted weapons. The Utelif paid them no attention at all.

"It's impossible. How are we going to get close enough to try and calm the Utelif?" Kimisi asked.

Suddenly, the beast turned sharply, its jagged horn catching one of the warrior's legs and leaving a gash.

The warrior cried out and the others gathered around their wounded sister protectively. The net dropped to the bottom of the lake as the Utelif charged towards them.

Jarell gripped the Staff of Kundi tightly. He had to do something. The water around them was growing darker from the wound on the warrior's leg, but he didn't want to hurt the Utelif either.

*You can do this!* Jarell thought. He called upon the Staff of Kundi. The warmth of the Iron

Leopard's fire radiated through him. He rocketed through the water like a torpedo, a tight circle of power wrapped around his body.

He needed to get to the warriors before the creature did. But the Utelif was fast. Jarell pushed his body harder than he ever thought possible. He felt fire surround him as he pulled the staff to his chest and zoomed in front of the warriors.

The large body of the beast stopped, flinching at the heat coming off Jarell. With a roar, it tumbled backwards into the darkness of the water.

The warriors kicked upwards, carrying their injured friend. Jarell and Kimisi followed. As they surfaced, another warrior robed in red and white extended a hand to help them both out.

"Are you all right, Jarell?" Kimisi asked as she climbed on to a lily pad. "I can't believe how fast you moved. Or how bright you shone."

Jarell wiped a hand over his face. It was trembling and he felt light-headed. It was as if he'd just run a marathon. Twice.

The warrior who had been injured lay on another lily pad next to them, unmoving. A warrior sister sat by her side.

"I should try and heal her," Jarell said. "I've healed before."

But before Kimisi or the other warrior could reply, the injured mermaid coughed. She sat up and her eyes swirled gold and turquoise. She tucked her braids behind her delicate grey fins that curved like ears. "I'm well enough, mortal," the warrior said. "But thank you."

"Are you sure you're OK?" Jarell asked, pressing the button on his visor so that it folded back.

The injured warrior gave a wave of her hand

with an impatient "*tsk*" noise.

"Don't be unkind, Aphia," the warrior next to her rebuked. "These two children were trying to help us. The boy has driven the Utelif away. For the moment, at least."

A wind suddenly sprung up, and the warriors all around them on the lily pads stood to attention.

"Tekanu comes," Aphia whispered, and she stood with the support of her friend.

"Who is Tekanu?" Jarell asked, turning to Kimisi.

Kimisi pointed across the lake at a swirling twister heading their way. "That is Tekanu."

# CHAPTER SIX

## THE BEAST IN THE RIVER

At the centre of the cyclone, on a throne of water, sat a woman dressed in a flowing blue robe and coral crown. She looked just as powerful as the storm goddess Ayana. Her long locs ran like a waterfall down her back.

"The River Mother of the merpeople," Kimisi's voice was a breath of awe.

Automatically, Jarell's visor shunted back over his face as a shooting pillar of water lifted the two of them up and towards the River Mother.

"Is this *Tekanu* on our side?" Jarell shouted, as he and Kimisi were dragged through the water.

"It's not that simple," Kimisi yelled back. "Tekanu claims no sides – she is neither an ally of Kundi nor Ikala. All that matters to her is protecting her own."

Jarell winced. If Tekanu had no friends, she had no loyalties. How could she be trusted?

Tekanu hovered above them, majestic on her throne of water. Seaweed decorated her hair and rainbow-coloured scales ran down the sides of her face and neck. "Mortals," she said from the top of her tower. Her voice was smooth like honey, yet held the power to wash them away. "What does the River Mother provide?"

Jarell shared a look with Kimisi. Kimisi shrugged.

"*Everything,*" her warriors answered in unison from down below. They stood to perfect attention on the lily pads, not moving a single muscle.

"Who would dare to defy Tekanu?" the River Mother demanded.

"*No one,*" her warriors responded.

"And what can stand in our way?" Tekanu roared.

"NOTHING!" her warriors cried.

Tekanu nodded to herself, seemingly satisfied. Jarell wondered if she was trying to impress them.

"Now you understand my power, mortals, do you think I look like someone who allows her business to be disrupted?"

"We were just trying to help," Jarell said. "That beast was—"

"Do not speak of the so-called *beast*," Tekanu snarled. "I order you both to stay out of our way." She swiped her hand and Jarell felt his body flying through the air. He landed on the bank of the lake with a thud. The impact robbed him of breath for a moment, but his pride hurt more than his body.

Kimisi flopped down next to him as the River Mother swept her arms in a wide arc and began gathering water from the lake. She formed it into a glistening orb between her fingertips and then cast it down into the lake.

The water parted. Jarell didn't know if it was magic or technology, but it was beautiful. The ball of power split the water in two, revealing the Utelif, who cowered on the bed of the lake. The orb then surrounded it in a shimmering bubble of bright blue water.

The Utelif growled at the warriors around

it, primed for another attack, but stopped the moment Tekanu met its gaze. To Jarell's surprise, the Utelif then seemed to relax. A rumbling sound of contentment came from the bubble.

Jarell watched in amazement as Tekanu floated towards the bubble, stepped inside and lovingly stroked the scales above the beast's eyes. She began to sing.

Jarell glanced at Kimisi to ask her a question, but the young griot stood mesmerized by Tekanu's singing. Jarell could feel the power of the River Mother's song. A calmness seemed to infuse everything around them.

The Utelif gave a low moan that almost sounded human, and then its eyes finally closed. Tekanu left the orb. She signalled to the mermaids and they threw their net over the sleeping beast. Then she turned to face Jarell and Kimisi on the bank.

"Jarell!" Kimisi whispered urgently. "Don't mention Ayana or Legsy to Tekanu . . . maybe not even your ancestor, Kundi. The River Mother will not care who sent us. Remember, she is friends with no one."

Tekanu floated across the water, her coral crown tall and regal, and her eyes glowing with rage.

"Unwanted visitors are a plague upon my waters," Tekanu said, coming to the edge of the lake. "A cursed plague that spreads fear and hurt."

Her sour tone reminded Jarell of his teacher when she'd really lost it. Jarell didn't get into trouble at school unless it was because he was drawing instead of paying attention in class.

"Explain your presence here," Tekanu demanded.

Jarell swallowed, wondering if he should let

Kimisi do the talking, but his companion seemed lost for words as well. The River Mother pointed at his staff, which was on his belt loop. Something in her expression changed. "The Staff of Kundi?" She sounded thoughtful.

"Yes." Jarell nodded.

Tekanu frowned. "But without all its Iron Animals. What has happened to them, do you suppose?"

He could hear the concern in the River Mother's voice. Kimisi had said that Tekanu didn't care for the battles of others, but perhaps there were things she *did* care about.

"Mother ... Tekanu ... of the River ..." Jarell answered. "The Iron Animals were scattered by ... by ..." Jarell remembered that Kimisi told him not to mention any specific names to Tekanu, but he wanted to tell the truth. "They were scattered by

Ayana and we are trying to collect them before they fall into the wrong hands."

Tekanu took a moment to consider this before turning slowly to Kimisi. "You are a warrior of Ayana."

"Zura Mohlo, Tekanu," Kimisi answered. "I am in Ayana's service, but I have pledged myself to help Jarell in this mission to find the Iron Animals."

"Yet I smell a trickster at work," Tekanu sniffed. "Is that how you got here?"

"I've been drawing these pictures," Jarell explained. "Pictures of the Manatees. They led us here—"

"Pah!" Tekanu laughed, a ripple of colour flowing across the scales on her neck. "The Manatees are peaceful, but senseless creatures. They know less than nothing."

"Well, Kimisi saw them in her seeing bowl too!"

Jarell replied defensively. "They hold the key to finding the Iron Crocodile. They led us here. The Iron Crocodile must be close."

Tekanu's expression became stony. "Let me look at the staff." She held out a webbed hand, but Jarell hesitated. *Can I trust her? Perhaps she is on Ikala's side. Perhaps Ikala will turn up any minute . . .*

A trickle of liquid spilled from one of her fingers and formed a curling snake of water that looped itself around the staff.

Jarell hesitated, but he finally let go of the staff.

"Kundi loved the water," Tekanu muttered, studying the staff as she drew it towards her. "He was perhaps too kind-hearted to rule, but he was a mighty warrior." She sighed. "I have never been one to make allies, and yet Kundi was the exception."

She glanced at them both and handed back the staff. The fierceness in her face had softened. Now Jarell noticed regret, like someone who simply missed a close friend.

Tekanu lifted her chin. "Help me, heir of Kundi, and the Iron Crocodile will be revealed. The blood in your veins tells me that you can do what I need." She turned to Kimisi. "And you, warrior of Ayana, will help him. Find the cure for the Utelif's curse, and the Iron Crocodile will show itself."

"The Utelif is cursed?" Kimisi asked, her tone confused.

"Yes, and the cure needs to be found" – Tekanu paused and Jarell could see the pain in her eyes – "before the Utelif destroys . . . or is destroyed."

"But how do we break the curse?" Jarell felt his hands curl into fists. He just wanted to find the

Iron Crocodile, but instead they were being given a whole new quest. What if Ikala found the Iron Crocodile first?

Tekanu shook her head. "That I cannot tell you. Now, GO!"

# CHAPTER SEVEN

## THE ABANDONED SEA FOREST

"Find the cure before the Utelif destroys or is destroyed . . ." Jarell muttered as they headed back underwater to find the Manatees. He turned to Kimisi. "It's not much to go on, is it? I mean, why couldn't she give us more information? And what is the curse?"

"The Ancients can be frustrating," Kimisi said,

"but Tekanu must have her reasons. The seeing bowl never lies. The Manatees are our best hope of finding out what to do next."

As the two of them swam upriver, Jarell was surprised to see that the big herd of Manatees had left, leaving only two grazing at the water's edge.

"Hello?" Jarell called out.

The two Manatees turned and bustled towards them. "Hi hi hi," they chimed again. "We waited for the sky ones to come on by!"

Jarell nodded. "What are your names, friends?"

The two Manatees spun around each other, humming. "Bool and Chip, Chip and Bool, those are the names we hear and call!"

Jarell grinned. "Jarell's my name and a quest is my game," he replied. "And this is Kimisi . . . she likes to eat sushi?" He trailed off. There was a reason why he never joined in when his brother was coming up with lyrics back at home in their shared bedroom.

"Jarell, this is not the time for silly rhymes." Kimisi's expression was stern. "And what in all of Ulfrika is *sushi*?" She held up a hand. "Tell me another time. We've got work to do."

Jarell nodded. "Look, friends," he began, "we are looking for a cure to break the curse of the Utelif. Do you know of anything that could help?"

"Cure?" said Bool. The Manatees' heads tilted, and their jet-black eyes flickered.

"Sure, sure, sure!" Chip added. He rolled over, revealing his plump belly. Jarell couldn't help but chuckle, and it looked like Kimisi was doing her best not to smile.

"It is the pearl pendant that can heal all!"

Bool said. More clicks and whistles came, but the translator couldn't make sense of it.

"What pearl?" Jarell asked.

The Manatees backed away. "Horses not seen, in grasses so green!"

"Horses ... Grasses ...?" Jarell didn't get it. *Why can't the Manatees say things normally?*

"Horses and grass are things found on land," Kimisi replied wearily.

"So we need to go above water for the cure?" Jarell added.

The Manatees growled, and that didn't need any translation.

*But if it's not above water, where is it?* Jarell wondered. His head was spinning. To find the Iron Crocodile, they had to find a cure for the Utelif. The cure was a pearl pendant, but that was hidden in the green grasses. No one had told him that being a Future Hero was going to be so complicated.

"Horses ride!" the Manatees said together. "Forests of the tide!"

"Wait. Could you be talking of the Inkya?" Kimisi asked.

Bool and Chip spun around excitedly. "Yes, yes," they sang. "Horses ride, forests of the tide!"

"Who are the Inkya?" asked Jarell.

Kimisi turned off her translator with a click, letting the Manatees drift off to graze on some stems on the riverbed.

"The Inkya are the Sea Horse people, Jarell. Even us griots aren't sure they are real, but there are many, many stories about them. It is said that if a traveller does anything to disrespect the sea, the Inkya take them to the Shadow Sea Forest – never to be seen again."

"So the Inkya have the pearl?" Jarell said. "The cure for the Utelif?"

Kimisi shrugged. "I hope so. But if we can't get that pearl from the Inkya, we have no way of curing the Utelif and no chance of Tekanu giving us the Iron Crocodile. And then . . ." Kimisi trailed off.

"And then Ikala the sorcerer will win," Jarell finished. "Well, where is this great underwater forest where the Inkya might live? We can't waste any more time."

Kimisi activated her power cuff. A bright blue hologram flickered into life, showing a coastline. There were no details of any sea forest on there. "Perhaps it really is just a story," she muttered.

Jarell sighed. What were they going to do? Tekanu was their best chance of getting the Iron Crocodile, but she wasn't going to help them until they helped her. And all the while Ikala was out there searching for the crocodile himself.

Jarell let his feet sink into the bed of the river. *Think. What would Kundi do?* Tekanu had thought the Manatees useless, but there must be a reason why Kimisi saw them in the seeing bowl and why Jarell had been drawing them. *Perhaps if we're to succeed we need to trust them completely.*

Jarell turned his translator back on. "Bool, Chip, can you take us to the Shadow Sea Forest?"

Bool and Chip swam back, nodding their heads. "Sure!" they sang. "We'll fly across the sea floor." They held out two long weeds to tow Jarell and Kimisi again.

Away from the pack, these young Manatees swam a bit faster. Singing happily, they plunged into an underground current, flowing in and out of caverns, swamps, and then out where the tree shrubs met the sea.

"Nice shortcut," Jarell said.

Kimisi laughed. "I'm thinking that Manatee is the only way to travel."

The water grew rougher as they hit the strong ocean waves. They'd passed the last coral reef a while ago. Now a vast seaweed forest loomed in front of them. Strong trunks as thick as armour and taller than mountains greeted them. An eerie mist of colourful light lurked just at the outer edge.

"I don't believe it!" Kimisi called over the radio in awe. "We found the Shadow Sea Forest!"

"It's amazing," Jarell whispered, as he felt an underwater current brush across his back. "Tell me more about the Inkya, Kimisi."

His friend frowned in concentration. "Legend says the Sea Horse folk are secretive, yet strong

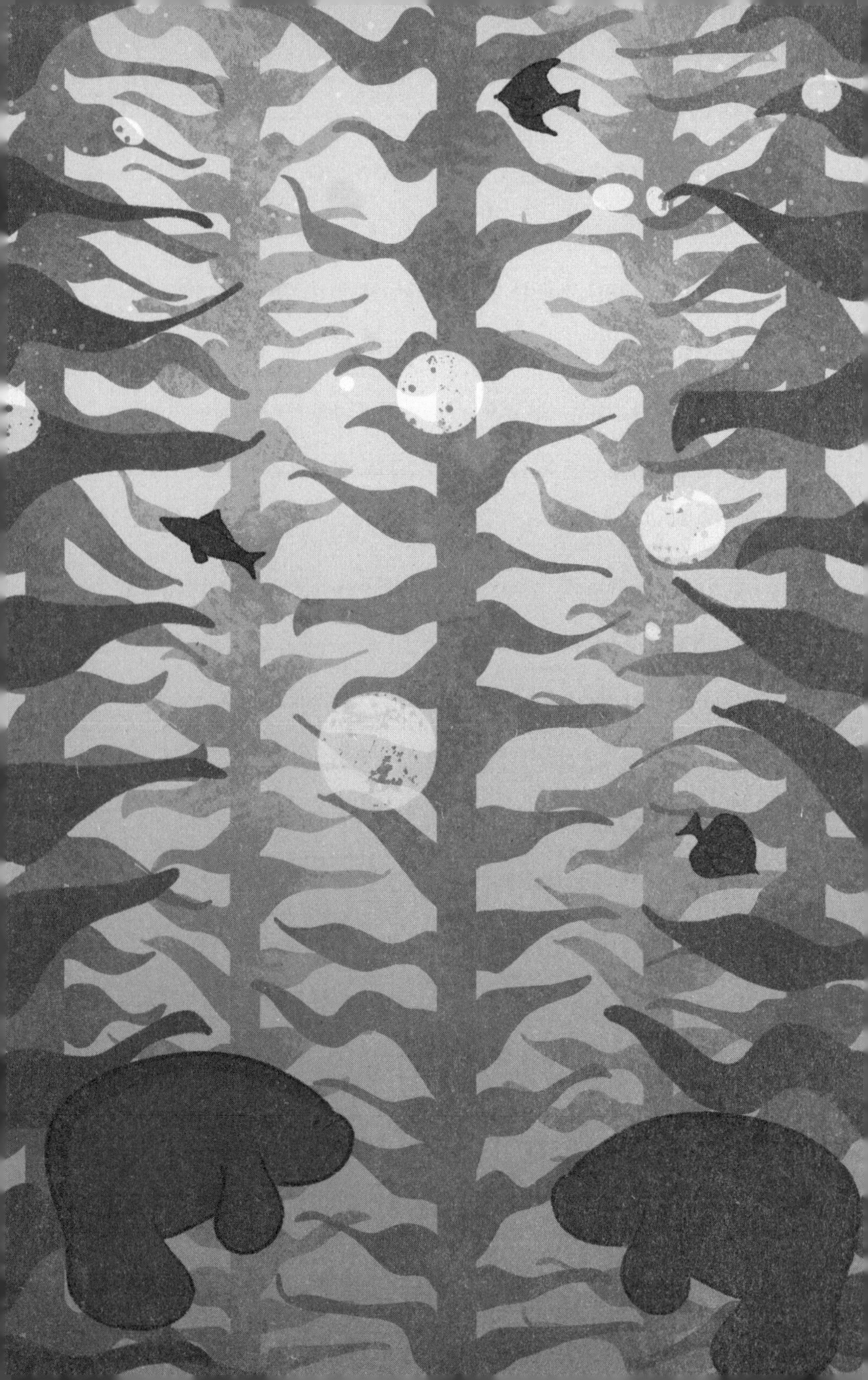

and powerful. They can grow to huge sizes – monstrous sizes – in the right conditions."

Bool and Chip brought them closer to the forest. Jarell and Kimisi let go of the weed reins. The Manatees started to sing again as they drifted away and grazed on some seaweed.

"How are we going to get through this forest?" Jarell asked. "Or find the pearl pendant to cure the Utelif?"

He watched as an eerie mist continued to grow at the edges of the forest. *I'll definitely have to draw that when I get back home . . .* If *I get home.*

The mist was suddenly so much closer. It wove itself into a tight circle that lassoed Bool and Chip like a cowboy would. The Manatees' song stopped. Their mouths were open in shock as they sank like stones to the bottom of the seabed.

"No!" Jarell yelled, unsure of what had just

attacked the Manatees.

The colourful mist tightened into a long tentacle and surged towards Kimisi and Jarell.

Kimisi charged with her spear, and Jarell grabbed his staff. The tentacle of mist stopped just a few metres away. By its glowing light, Jarell could see the pulse of the current that separated them from the strange mist creature.

"The current!" Kimisi called out. "It's keeping the mist away from us. Swim into the current!"

They fell into the current's slipstream and watched as the tentacle of mist reared back as if it had been burned, disappearing into the darkness.

Jarell and Kimisi shot towards Bool and Chip. They lay very still on the seabed.

"They've been turned to stone," Kimisi said. "Poor things."

The Manatees lay on the sea floor, too heavy

for even the current to move. Their skin had turned completely dark grey and crusty, and their jet-black eyes were completely still.

Jarell hovered his hands over their bodies. He tried to feel the connection with his ancestral powers to heal them, focusing his mind just like he had to heal his friend Chinell, the Painted Wolf, in his first visit to Ulfrika. But there was something different this time. Jarell could sense nothing except the knowledge that this was beyond the healing powers even his ancestors had possessed. He was helpless.

"Jarell, we need to go before it returns," Kimisi urged.

"We can't just leave them like this," Jarell cried. "They're our friends."

"Wait! They told us that the pearl heals, and we know it breaks curses. The pendant might be able to help them too," she replied. "But if we're turned to stone, no one will be saving anyone." She fished out two discs from her belt. "Here – these are tracking beacons. Once we have the cure, we'll be able to find them again."

Jarell nodded reluctantly as Kimisi attached the discs to the Manatees' rock-hard back flippers. "We'll be back for you," he whispered to his new friends, who lay as still as statues. "I promise."

Jarell and Kimisi entered the forest. They could not glide in between the giant seaweed stalks like the deadly mist. Instead, they had to hack at the weeds with their spear and staff.

Jarell soon realized that the bright-green seaweed was the strongest. It took ages to cut. But the browner seaweed with the rougher outer shell was the weakest. Some of those seaweed stalks were dead and could be cut with his staff in a single swipe. Together, Jarell and Kimisi cut deeper and deeper into the weeds until they found a gap in the centre of the dense forest. It was wide enough for them to stand side by side. Two paths stretched out in front of them.

"Someone definitely made these paths," Jarell said. "They've got to go somewhere."

"What if they lead somewhere we don't want to go?" Kimisi asked.

"Well, if you don't turn the corner, you can't know what's ahead," said Jarell. "That's what my granddad always told us."

"That sounds like an Ulfrikan saying for sure." Kimisi stared at both paths. "Let's take the left path," she said. "It looks like it goes deeper into the forest."

They set off. The path twisted and curved but did not seem to end. Curious crabs and little fish poked out of the dense seaweed that surrounded them, and then swiftly hid themselves again.

Finally the path led them into a clearing where a tall building made of rough red and orange coral stretched upwards. It had holes for doors and windows, but as they swam closer, Jarell could only see darkness inside.

Jarell scanned the building up and down. His throat suddenly felt dry. What were they going to discover in there? *There's only one way to find out*, he told himself.

Jarell looked at Kimisi. "Shall we go in?"

# CHAPTER EIGHT

## ON THE RUN

"Of course we'll go in." Kimisi tapped a button on Jarell's power cuff and then one on hers.

Jarell's whole cuff vibrated and a bright white light shone from it. Kimisi's cuff also lit up, illuminating her body and everything around her. As they swam through the doorway, Jarell felt his insides twist viciously with nerves. He glanced at

Kimisi, but she looked completely calm. He wished he felt the same.

Inside the building, the walls were decorated with swirls of multicoloured sand. The closer he looked, the more Jarell could see in the splashes of colour. The wall was telling a story. *I wish I could draw this*, Jarell thought. He would try and remember every detail for his next drawing.

"Jarell, you'd better come here," Kimisi called. "I think I've found the Inkya."

Jarell hadn't even noticed Kimisi had gone, but he spotted the light from her cuff further down a long hallway. He swam after her and into another room.

Seven statues sat at a circular table, bodies covered in fine stripes and dressed in armour and gold. Despite having fins, long horse-like muzzles and powerful-looking serpent tails, they sat like humans at the table.

*Actually, like* scared *humans at the table,* Jarell thought. *They look just like Bool and Chip did when they got turned to stone.*

"That mist," Jarell breathed. "The mist did this. We have to help them."

"We cannot save everyone, Jarell," Kimisi replied. "We have to focus and find that pearl pendant. You don't want to be the warrior who wins little victories but loses the war."

"What do you mean?" said Jarell.

Kimisi sighed. "If we save every creature we come across, we might lose sight of our real quest. Finding the Iron Animals and defeating Ikala."

"But if we don't try, then we're no better than Ikala," Jarell explained.

"Baku!" Kimisi muttered under her breath. "You sound like Kundi from the old tales. There is a story, actually, about Kundi and the In—" Kimisi broke off. "Wait! What is that?"

In the corner of a dark chamber, Jarell spotted a shape in the shadows. As he swam closer, he saw that it was a lone Inkya. The poor creature had been turned into stone from his tail to his chest, but one of his arms was still free.

The Inkya bared his teeth. "Wh-who are you?" he growled, raising a spear with his free arm.

Jarell attached his staff to his belt loop. "My name is Jarell. This is Kimisi." He held up his arms to show that he meant no harm. "What's your name?"

"Sonbi," the Inkya muttered, narrowing his eyes.

"Nice to meet you, Sonbi. We're here to help. We know what has happened to you and your friends."

"The Zin has happened. Even though we have not seen its kind for generations!" Sonbi's voice cracked with emotion. "It is that sorcerer's fault, I'm sure."

*"Sorcerer?"* Jarell and Kimisi said at the same time. "Do you mean Ikala?"

Sonbi nodded. "Ikala was here. Asking us if we'd seen the Iron Crocodile. When I said no, he left and I thought that was the end of it. Then the Zin appeared. Ikala made that happen." Sonbi's eyes were large.

"You must help me get to our city. Maybe the pearl will hel—" Sonbi broke off, eyes widening at something behind them.

Jarell and Kimisi spun around. An eerie glowing mist filled the doorway.

"The Zin has come for us!" Sonbi screamed.

Kimisi grabbed her spear and banged it against the crushed coral floor to charge it. Twirling it around her head, she sent a blast into the middle of the mist, punching a hole straight through it, but the mist quickly filled the gap again and crept forward.

Jarell grabbed the Staff of Kundi and he felt the iron vibrate in his palm. He tumbled out of the way as the mist transformed into a tentacle and lashed out at him.

"Jarell, Kimisi, go! Leave me," Sonbi cried. "Warn my people about the Zin. Find the pearl in the city."

The Zin sprang at Sonbi like a snake and the Inkya was turned completely into stone.

"No!" Jarell cried. Staggering to his feet, he sent a flare of fire from the Staff of Kundi. The Zin flowed around the pulse, growing denser and brighter as it absorbed his weapon's power.

Kimisi grabbed Jarrell's arm and pulled him towards the window. "Come on," she cried. "We've got to get out of here."

"But we can't just leave Sonbi!" he cried.

"Jarell, we can't take down the Zin here. Come on."

Jarell turned and escaped out of the window after her. There was nothing they could do for Sonbi at the moment. He knew that.

There was a low gusting sound from behind him, and Jarell looked over his shoulder to see the

Zin following them. It sent out a mass of mist-like tentacles like a giant squid.

"OK, listen," Kimisi said. "We should split up. It gives us twice the chance of getting to the Inkya's city and finding the pearl pendant. At least we now know that it really exists." She chewed her lip. "If we stick together, we might both end up as stone statues."

"Are you sure that's the right decision?" Jarell asked. "Ikala is the one who made the Zin appear. It's going to be super powerful."

Kimisi shrugged. "I cannot be sure of anything right now. The Ancient I serve is still unwell. Ayana told me that I can no longer trust those in my compound. That they may be in Ikala's thrall." Kimisi shook her head. "I cannot go home until we find all the Iron Animals and defeat Ikala – that's the hard choice I make every day. Splitting up now is just one more hard choice."

Jarell nodded. Kimisi might at times pretend to be as tough as stone, but the truth was far more complicated. His friend was giving up a lot to be on this quest. "Be safe, Kimisi," Jarell said.

"You too, heir of Kundi," replied Kimisi with a sad smile.

Jarell kicked off towards a path he could see at the edge of the clearing. He turned his head and saw that the Zin had already split in two, part of it following Kimisi as she disappeared down another path.

The other half was following him.

The Zin darted towards his legs, and Jarell found himself remembering the Ingalo moves that Legsy taught him. Jarell tucked his legs in and used his momentum to roll in the water.

*Ingalo is understanding the rhythm of your*

*opponent's movements, responding before they can strike,* Jarell reminded himself. He let go of any hope of hurting the Zin, but concentrated on avoiding the tendrils of mist trying to strike at him.

Jarell ducked and weaved, edging further down the path as the Zin gained on him. But the Zin was tiring. Jarell was sure of it. Its tendrils were not reaching as far or moving as fast as before.

As Jarell turned a corner, he checked over his shoulder and realized that the Zin was nowhere to be seen.

Jarell activated his radio. "Kimisi, can you hear me?" he whispered. "I've lost the Zin. How're you doing?"

"Speak up, Jarell. I think you might be out of range." Kimisi's voice crackled over the radio. "If you can hear this, I think I've managed t—"

Suddenly, Jarell could hear the gusting sound

of the Zin through the radio.

"No, it's still following me!" Kimisi cried. "I think it's picking up on my transmission. I've got to go. You find that pearl."

His headpiece went silent. Kimisi was gone. *Should I go back?* he asked himself. *We came to do this together.* But Jarell knew that Kimisi would want him to keep going. He had to make the hard choice.

Jarell swam down the path, listening out for the Zin. As he went further, the giant kelp on either side formed a dark arch over his head and snagged at his body. It felt like he was being swallowed up by it.

*I wish Kimisi was here. I wish I wasn't alone . . .*

*You are never alone, Jarell,* a deep voice whispered inside him. It was the voice of his ancestor, Kundi. It sent ripples of hope through him like a stone thrown into a pond.

"I've left Kimisi behind, and I don't know if that was the right choice," he whispered. "And the Zin is too powerful. It's working for Ikala. Even the staff didn't work against it."

*When I was a child, people told me I was weak,* Kundi told him. *I believed them for a long time too. Until I realized that strength comes from our choices and doing the right thing. Kimisi is strong. As are you. You will find a way to defeat the Zin, this puppet of Ikala's.*

Kundi's words gave Jarell renewed strength to his arms and legs and he surged forwards. Soon the path ended, and a city of coral expanded out in front of him. *The home of the Inkya.*

At the centre of the city, behind an elaborate fountain of bubbles, stood a palace. Its turrets sparkled with sea glass. Swaying kelp fronds fanned

out from the corners of windows. The palace was beautiful. But the city was empty.

Where were the Inkya Sea Horse people who Jarell promised he would warn?

Had the Zin been here already?

"Sonbi," Jarell said out loud. "I'm so sorry. I've failed."

# CHAPTER NINE

## THE FROZEN ARMY

Jarell glided through the city like a ghost and headed for the palace. If anyone was left in the city, maybe they would be there.

He had barely swum in through the door when he found his first group of Inkya, frozen in a frightened huddle. The further he went, the more Inkya he found: Inkya soldiers trying to make barricades, servants hurrying about, and ordinary citizens seeking shelter. The coral throne was empty. Every frozen face was fearful. *The Zin has done this.*

Jarell examined the throne, finding no sign of anyone or the pearl pendant.

Had the royalty who once sat here escaped the Zin? Or was the Zin not even the enemy Jarell should be worried about?

*Why is the Zin attacking the Inkya?* Jarell asked himself. *Is it punishing everyone because Ikala couldn't find the Iron Crocodile?* Jarell ground his teeth. Ikala was a bully. And Jarell hated bullies.

Jarell went outside to think, away from all the stone Inkya. He stood by the fountain of bubbles and opened up the headset's channel. "What is it you always say, Kimisi? Two heads are better than one. Unless you are facing a Ninki-Nanka, of course."

The transmitter simply buzzed with static in response.

"She's all right," Jarell told himself. "She has to be." Still, a vision of Kimisi frozen in stone filled his mind.

"Jarell!"

Kimisi's voice echoed around his helmet and Jarell felt a knot in his stomach loosen.

She spoke again. "By Ayana's will, it is good to hear your voice, Jarell!"

"Are you OK? Where are you? How did you escape?"

"Eh, how do you expect any answer if you ask all your questions at once?" Kimisi replied with a laugh. "I'm fine. I remembered how the clever snake escaped the sun by crawling under a rock. I saw a crack in the ground and slipped away before the Zin could see where I'd gone. I followed the crack into a cavern. Sure, I got a little lost, but I found my way out. No sign of the Zin now. What about you?"

Jarell told Kimisi what had happened to him, and how he was now in the city of coral.

"Good," Kimisi said. "I'll try and find you. We need to get back to Tekanu with that pearl. Remember, she said the Utelif will 'destroy or be destroyed' if we don't break the curse. Time is running out."

Jarell nodded and once more began scouring the city for any traces of life. "I know. If we don't break the curse she won't give us the Iron Crocodile. But I'm looking, and there is no one to even ask. Everyone has been turned to stone."

"It's a shame your ancestor can't give you a clue," Kimisi replied over the airways.

Jarell frowned. "It's not really like that. Kundi

speaks to me whenever I need to hear him most. But I can't just call him up."

"I'm just saying, it would be great if he could give us some information. From what I remember in the legends, Kundi visited this city."

"Wait! Kundi knew this place? He knew the Inkya?" Jarell stopped in his tracks. "Why didn't you tell me?"

"I tried, but we were a bit busy trying to survive the Zin," Kimisi said patiently. "In the time before the staff was at its most powerful, the legend says Kundi and his trusted followers set off to visit a great shapeshifter living on an island off the coast of Ulfrika. They set sail in calm weather but soon hit trouble."

"A storm?" Jarell asked.

"A storm? No . . . that would make for a very boring story," Kimisi replied. "Good thing I'm the griot here. No, an ancient sea creature known as the Walé swallowed them whole." Her voice became softer. He could tell she was enjoying telling this story. "Kundi's followers had to light a fire in the Walé to be free. It cried out in pain and spat them out."

"Kundi wouldn't have liked that," Jarell murmured. In the distance he could see a fountain of bubbles. He moved towards it.

"Who is telling this story?" Kimisi demanded. "But you are right. Kundi felt the Walé didn't deserve to live in pain, so he went to the Inkya King for his pearl, which was famed for its healing powers."

Jarell thought of how similar this story was to their mission. It was only by obtaining the pearl that they would heal the Utelif and find the Iron Crocodile.

Kimisi continued. "Appreciating Kundi's compassion, the Sea Horse people took the pearl pendant from the middle of their *Biougware*. It was unheard of—"

"Hold on, Kimisi," Jarell interrupted. "Where did they get the pendant from?"

"Their *Biougware*," Kimisi repeated.

"And what's that?" he asked.

"Umm, I believe it's an ancient Inkyan word." Kimisi sounded unsure, a little embarrassed. "Even my mother's mother wasn't certain. She thought it meant Tower of Skies . . . no . . . Tower of Breath? It probably never existed. Anyway, are you going to let me finish the story?"

Jarell's eyes fixed on the fountain of bubbles that towered over him. "Wait one minute, Kimisi. I think I've found the Tower of Breath."

He knelt down. Parts of the fountain were

clearly recent, but most of the coral was bleached white with age. Could it have been here that Kundi visited the Inkya? Knowing Kundi had been here somehow made it seem so right that a boy from South London was his heir. Like their lives crossed where it mattered.

"*Well?*" Kimisi asked over the headset.

Jarell climbed on to the fountain and tried to reach into its heart. Bubbles surged against him and spat him back out on to the crushed coral floor.

"Ouch," he yelped.

"What's happening?" Kimisi demanded. "Are you OK?"

"I'm fine. It's just that the fountain is not really up for visitors."

"Baku! You need me there, but I'm still swimming down some random path."

"It's OK. I've got this." Jarell climbed on the

fountain again, this time summoning the power of the Iron Leopard to move with lightning speed. He slipped through the mass of bubbles and into a narrow secret chamber. The stone walls were laced with golden seaweed that gave off a soft glow.

"Whoa," Jarell breathed.

"Is that a good whoa or a bad whoa, Jarell?" Kimisi asked with concern.

"A good whoa, Kimisi!" Jarell replied, spinning in awe at the brightness around him, Kundi's staff vibrating in his hand. "I'm in some kind of chamber."

Carefully, he moved deeper towards the centre of the chasm. He was getting closer to something powerful. He could feel it. A patch of golden seaweed caught his eye. *It's a different shade than the rest,* he realized, brushing it aside. His fingers felt something metallic and he pulled out a golden chain with a large pearl at its centre.

The pendant felt right in his hands – as if it recognized him, or his ancestry. He suddenly felt sure that the legend of Kundi using it was true.

"I found it, Kimisi," he yelled through the radio. "Tekanu has to tell us where the Iron Crocodile is now!"

As he raced back to the fountain, he imagined himself with the Iron Crocodile on the Staff of Kundi. If he had two Iron Animals, he would be halfway through his quest to stop Ikala and bring the staff back to its full strength.

"I found you!" Kimisi's voice called as Jarell emerged from the fountain.

Jarell spotted Kimisi waiting for him, one hand on her hip and a face that beamed with pride behind her visor. "Good thing I told you that Kundi story, eh?" she teased. "Come, we must get back to Tekanu and the Iron Crocodile."

Jarell nodded but stopped as he spotted one of the frozen Inkyas standing just a few steps away. They were holding a baby Inkya in their arms.

"Wait, Kimisi. We can't leave the Inkyas this way. We have to return them to normal and help them defeat the Zin."

"But we have a quest to complete," Kimisi said impatiently.

"I know," Jarell replied. "But don't you see that it's all connected? Ikala is the one who has brought the Zin upon the Inkya. We need to defeat it." Jarell winced, waiting for Kimisi to tell him that he needed to focus on their quest. But instead Kimisi was looking at him with deep respect.

"Go on then," she said. "Let's hear your plan."

*

After arriving back at the palace, Jarell and Kimisi worked together to find every single Inkya. They swam through windows, grand rooms and halls, and freed each Inkya using the pearl pendant. Fearful stony gazes transformed into faces full of joy. Families cried and nuzzled noses as they were reunited.

The Sea Horse people gathered in the city's centre as Jarell and Kimisi told them of how they were going to get rid of the Zin once and for all.

"We don't know much about the Zin, but we do know that it cannot survive in strong ocean currents. It breaks up," Jarell explained.

"It's because the Zin is made from thousands of tiny creatures," one of the Inkya explained. "On their own they are not dangerous, but together . . ." He shuddered. "Something . . . *someone* brought them together."

Jarell and Kimisi shared a look.

"Sonbi told us that the sorcerer Ikala is behind the Zin," Kimisi revealed. "But by Ayana's will, neither shall terrorize you any more."

"We need to go back to the forest," Jarell said. "Back to where the currents are the strongest."

Jarell and Kimisi led the way. Jarell soon realized they were very close to where Sonbi had been turned to stone.

"I think it's time to get some reinforcements," Jarell said.

With the pendant still around his neck, he slipped inside the coral building, unfreezing the Inkya around the table before healing Sonbi, who lay frozen in the shadows.

Sonbi blinked himself awake as Jarell slipped the pearl pendant back in his pocket. "You freed me," Sonbi said. "I owe you a great debt."

"It was the right thing to do," Jarell replied.

"Where are my people now? Have you freed them also?"

"The rest of your people are free." Jarell nodded. "And they are waiting for us to join them."

For a moment, Sonbi looked puzzled.

"It's a long story, and it is not finished yet," Jarell answered, extending out his hand to his new comrade. "Come and help us get rid of the Zin."

*

*Awoooooooo!*

A loud horn blasted to welcome them as Jarell and Sonbi approached the Inkya army.

Kimisi nodded at Sonbi. "It's good to see you again. Are you ready to face the Zin? The scout says it is coming this way."

Jarell felt his stomach flip. He had convinced the Inkya to fight, and he hoped that it was the right thing to do. But what if they lost the battle?

Sonbi beat a fist against his chest. "I am ready." He put a hand on Jarell's shoulder. "And so are you."

"And so am I," Jarell repeated, bringing a fist to his chest.

Kimisi did the same.

The other Inkyas followed Kimisi's action until the whole army held a fist to their chest.

Jarell's skin tingled. He felt the zing of everyone's nervous energy all around him. They all knew the plan. He just hoped it would work.

The army stood almost motionless; only the Sea Horses' fins fluttered rapidly to keep them afloat. All eyes were facing ahead.

Jarell heard that strange gusting sound again, and then the eerie mist appeared at the edge of the seaweed stems, larger than Jarell had ever seen it. Jarell heard a few Inkyas bray in terror as the Zin curled itself into a ball and hurled itself towards them.

"Now!" Jarell yelled.

Instantly, the Inkya army divided into three. The Zin was confused, but for only a second before it split itself into three to attack.

Jarell led his third of the army towards a jet of strong currents. Jarell could feel the slipstream gliding over his wetsuit and visor. He held out the Staff of Kundi and shot a flare of fire into the stream. Like an insect hovering around a light bulb, the Zin followed the fire straight into the current. It instantly broke up in the sea, being torn to ribbons before dissolving completely.

Some Inkyas to the left let out a loud cry of triumph and Jarell turned to see another fragment of the Zin dissolve on an ocean current.

That just left Kimisi's part of the army. Jarell watched his friend as she stood very still. The Zin crept towards her. Jarell felt himself wanting to cry out, but he stopped himself. At the very last moment, just when the last fragment of Zin was upon her, Kimisi backflipped into the slipstream. The Zin followed. It thrashed against the current as it was caught up, but it was no use. It burst into an explosion of bright colours before being swept away.

The Zin was gone.

# CHAPTER TEN

## NEW FRIENDS AND ENEMIES

As the Inkya roared in celebration, Sonbi took Jarell and Kimisi aside. With a broad smile, he patted them both on the shoulder.

"I cannot thank you enough for what you've done for my people," Sonbi said. "Without you two warriors, we'd still be statues and the Zin would still roam free."

"You know, it was the pendant that unfroze you." Jarell reached into the pocket of his dive suit and pulled out the pearl. He paused for a moment with it in his hands. Giving the pearl back would be the honourable thing to do, but if he did that, Tekanu would not show them where the Iron Crocodile was.

"Jarell, you aren't thinking of giving that pearl away, are you?" Kimisi hissed under her breath. "Put it back in your pocket and let's get out of here and find Tekanu."

Jarell thought of the story of Kundi and the Walé. Sometimes doing the right thing resulted in an even better outcome . . .

"There is a hero's way to do things," Jarell answered Kimisi. "You taught me that with the stories of Kundi. The pendant isn't ours to just take." He held out the pearl.

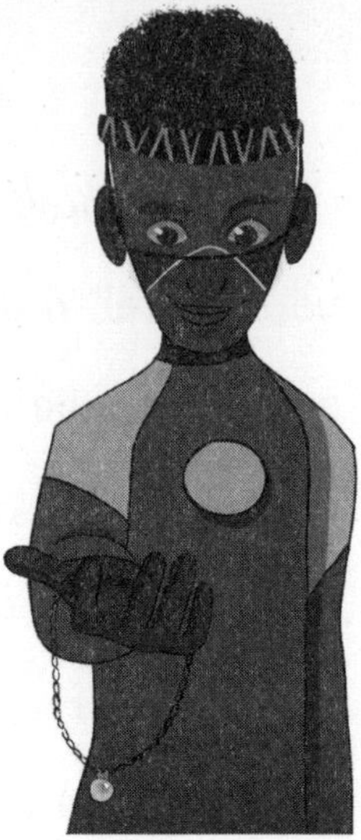

But Sonbi did not reach out to take it. "Tell me, what does your friend mean when she says you need to give this pearl to Tekanu?" Sonbi's face was serious. "The River Mother is not a friend. Our people are not welcome in her kingdom, and she is not welcome in ours."

Jarell hesitated, wondering if Kimisi was right after all. *Trust your instincts, just like Kundi trusted his. Tell him why it matters.*

"We are on a quest to restore the Staff of Kundi and find the Iron Crocodile before Ikala can," Jarell explained. "Tekanu knows where the Iron Crocodile is. She'll give it to us, but only if we bring her the pearl pendant to lift a curse from the Utelif terrorizing her lake."

He offered the pendant to Sonbi again. "Still, we have no right to just take this."

Sonbi glanced over at the Inkya swimming and hugging in celebration nearby. "My people need the pendant – it doesn't just stop the Zin or lift curses, it heals everyday illnesses," he replied. "But Ikala's evil is a sickness that it cannot cure."

"And he's a sickness that I must stop," Jarell finished.

"Exactly," Sonbi said. "Or we will all suffer."

"You speak truth, Sonbi," Kimisi said. "Griots speak of what he may do to other lands and other people. His greed is endless."

"Our griot has seen the same thing," Sonbi admitted. "Jarell, the Staff of Kundi has always held great power, but it needs to be wielded by a hero. You are that Future Hero, and I believe you can stop Ikala. Thanks to you and Kimisi, the Inkya people of the Shadow Sea Forest are free. Will you take the pearl pendant with our blessing to Tekanu?"

Jarell's chest felt tight with pride. Sonbi believed in him. "Are you sure?" Jarell asked.

"Baku! Don't try to talk him out of it." Kimisi shook her head.

Sonbi chuckled. "There is no chance of that. In the past we have not been the *closest* of allies with the River Mother, but today you have shown us the importance of helping our neighbours. If Tekanu is willing to send the pendant back when it is no longer needed, then perhaps our people can become friends once again." Sonbi nodded his head. "Go. You have a quest to complete."

Jarell and Kimisi waved goodbye to the Inkya and swam back through the great kelp forest. "Next stop, Tekanu," said Jarell.

Kimisi cleared her throat. "Not that I want to

slow us down, but we have got some Manatees to unfreeze!"

Jarell laughed. "Kimisi, are you getting as soft as me?"

"Perhaps. I spent a lot of time with those Manatees before you turned up." Kimisi struck out through the water. "Besides, Chip and Bool can always give us a ride."

They swam down the path they had cut earlier through the forest and soon Jarell and Kimisi found Bool and Chip, lying on the ground where they had left them. Jarell gently touched them with the pearl pendant.

The Manatees rose from the seabed and greedily began chomping on

kelp again.

*Looks like being statues was hard work,* Jarell thought.

"Hey, you two! We don't have time for snacks." Kimisi whistled.

"Sky ones, did you not succeed, or Chip and Bool do you still need?" they chirped.

"We're not quite finished yet," Jarell replied. "We've got a river goddess to meet. Can you help get us to her quickly?"

Bool and Chip gathered up some seaweed reins and swam over to them. Then they were off again. As they raced through the water, the sea landscape a blur of coral and jewel-coloured fish, Jarell couldn't make sense of his emotions. They had the pendant, but a worm of worry kept twisting through him. They needed to get that Iron Crocodile, and that was all dependent on fierce

Tekanu.

It wasn't long before they reached the secret underwater tunnel and were then back in the freshwater lake.

Jarell turned to the Manatees. "You should leave. I don't know how this next part is gonna go."

Bool nodded, but his eyes looked sad.

"Not if, but when. Chip and Bool will see you again," Chip said, staring at Kimisi and Jarell.

Kimisi stroked the Manatee's head. "Of that I'm sure."

"Good luck, sky ones, good luck." And then the Manatees were gone.

"Jarell, we must be careful," Kimisi said. "There are many stories that tell how Tekanu's mood can change rapidly. What will we do if she decides *not* to give us the Iron Crocodile?"

The same worry had been tickling the back of

Jarell's mind. What if Tekanu didn't hold up her end of the bargain?

"I'm choosing to believe that she will," he replied. "People change. Tekanu is the Inkyas' enemy, and they still gave us the pearl."

"Baku, you should pay more attention to the stories of the ancestors," Kimisi scolded. "Betrayal is not rare in Ulfrika. Even Kundi had his fair share of traitors."

Jarell thought back to how Raheem had offered to cover for him, even as Marc and Kadon had run off to get their ball. People could change.

"We will judge her on what she does today, not what she did in the past." Jarell grinned. "Wow! I sound so wise."

Kimisi rolled her eyes. The transmitter in their visors started to crackle. "Something is coming our way."

Jarell felt his stomach knot. *Is it the River Mother*?

The water around them started to glow. Tekanu's warriors looked as formidable as ever as they swam towards them.

"You are to follow us," the guards announced, before spreading out around Jarell and Kimisi.

"Great!" Jarell said. "We've got something for the River Mother."

One of the warriors smiled, but it did not reach her eyes. "Good. She has something for you too."

Jarell and Kimisi were led across the lakebed until they reached a city that grew out of the silty ground like a giant tree – except it was covered in pulsing electrical blue circuits. It was bigger than any skyscraper Jarell had seen in London. Arms of the city stretched out like branches with large pods

at the tip of each one. The skin of the pods was translucent as they flexed and shifted.

Jarell felt a firm push on his shoulder as the warriors steered them upwards to a pair of ornate doors that led into one of the pods. As they approached, the doors swished open and they entered a huge hall filled with merpeople.

Tekanu sat high on her throne, talking to an aide. She raised her hand and the hall fell silent. The crowd parted so Jarell and Kimisi could be led forward.

Approaching the River Mother, Jarell noticed that Tekanu almost looked worried. The impressive River Mother he'd met earlier was gone. Her coral crown wasn't on straight and her locs covered one side of her face. She clutched a tablet a little too tightly in her hands.

The guards crossed spears in front of them to

stop them getting any closer.

"You return." The River Mother's words echoed around the hall. "What do you bring?"

Jarell bowed. "We have kept our word," he said, pulling the pendant from his pocket. "The healing pearl in exchange for the Iron Crocodile."

Tekanu let out a hollow laugh. "You think the Iron Crocodile is mine to give? I didn't promise it, only that I would reveal its location. The deal was for information only. You should listen more carefully next time."

Jarell's hand closed over the pearl. Its cool smoothness was the direct opposite of the hot, rough rage building in his chest.

Kimisi pushed past Jarell. "And so the stories are true. You cannot be trusted. I knew it!"

Jarell saw Tekanu's warriors step forwards with their tridents, poised for attack. Perhaps Kimisi's show of anger wasn't the best idea while they were surrounded.

"Calm down, Kimisi," Jarell begged.

Kimisi turned to him. "But she lied to us, Jarell!" Kimisi said with fury. "How can she choose to play word games when the fate of Ulfrika is at stake? She doesn't understand—"

A sharp gust of wind whipped through the hall, cutting Kimisi off mid-sentence.

"You are the one who doesn't understand," the River Mother boomed. She narrowed her eyes. "Take them to the cell."

# CHAPTER ELEVEN

## THE LIE AND THE LULLABY

The guards led Jarell and Kimisi out behind the throne and down a spiral staircase. They plunged into a long narrow shaft that seemed to go deep beneath the lakebed.

Jarell cursed himself, wondering what they could do. *We were fools to trust the River Mother.*

A soft glowing light appeared at the bottom

of the shaft. The guards ahead of him swam out to a giant chamber in the rocks. Suspended in the middle of the underwater chamber, red laser-beams formed a huge cage.

*Why do they need such a big prison for us?* Jarell wondered. *This cell is so big it could hold a shark or something.* He slowed down to get a better look, but in the dim light, he couldn't see far inside it. The guard behind pushed him on.

More warriors were posted around the cavern, staring intently into the cage. They weren't stony-faced like Tekanu's warriors in the hall. Their expressions reminded Jarell of the look his mother had that time when his brother was about to be taken off by ambulance after falling off his bike – a deep love and worry. And they were singing.

*None of this makes sense.*

"That song," Kimisi whispered over the radio.

"It's so beautiful."

Jarell's headset was filled with the most wonderful harmonies. The chant rose and fell like the tides and was filled with the power of crashing waves. He didn't need to run the translator to appreciate how sad it was.

Then, out of the dark, the Utelif crashed against the inside of the cage, sending a shower of sparks across the chamber. Despite its reckless fury, it was clear it was also in pain.

"It is a lullaby," Kimisi murmured. "Of course, to calm the Utelif! And the words . . . I understand most of them. They're telling a story. I think the Utelif was once a merperson."

"You are correct," a voice said behind them.

Tekanu swam into the chamber and over to the cage. She reached out to touch the bars but then dropped her hand. Instead she stared sadly

at the Utelif.

"Jarell, Ikala came here looking for the Iron Crocodile," Kimisi said, listening closely to the singing. She paused before translating again. "He knew it was here. His magic told him."

There was a crash as the Utelif barged into the side of the cage and the River Mother took a step back.

Kimisi stared at Tekanu, her eyes wide. "The River Mother sent a messenger to refuse Ikala's demands. She would not reveal where the Iron Crocodile was. So Ikala cursed the merpeople . . . He cursed Tekanu's son to become a Utelif."

The River Mother turned to face them, the expression on her face one of complete defeat.

"That's your *son*?!" Jarell exclaimed. He instantly regretted the tone of his voice. Tekanu's tears spilled over. She looked so vulnerable.

"Why didn't you tell us?" Jarell asked. "We would have helped anyway."

"My silence was part of the curse," Tekanu said. "Ikala's cruelty knows no bounds."

Jarell closed his eyes. *The people in these underwater kingdoms have been put through so much, and it's all because of Ikala. Always Ikala.*

"I am a fool," Kimisi said, turning to Jarell.

"Ikala has cast this wicked curse before – it is in the legends. All part of the games he likes to play."

"I just wanted to save my son," the River Mother said in a quiet, broken voice.

Jarell swam up to Tekanu. "Here," he said, holding out the pearl pendant.

Tekanu smiled and took it. "Thank you, heir of Kundi. Thank you, Jarell."

The glowing bars of the cage parted for her as she swam into the cage. "No one is to interfere. My son is scared enough already." She held the pendant out and called for the river prince.

Out of the darkness, the Utelif shot towards her like a torpedo and Tekanu barely managed to get out of the way of its enormous jagged horn. The Utelif let out a deep, mournful cry before it smashed against the bars in a shower of sparks. He rammed the cage again and again with his horn. The laser bars flickered.

The lullaby stopped as the warriors looked around nervously. "Those bars won't hold," one warrior said.

"It is fine!" Tekanu shouted. "I just need him to be still." She darted forward, narrowly avoiding her son's ferocious swipes as she tried to get close enough to heal him. She was just an arm's length away when the Utelif whipped his tail, flinging the River Mother to the side of the cage. The pendant flew from her hand, and with a splutter the laser bars disappeared.

Instantly, the tridents of every warrior in the room glowed as their owners charged them up. "Protect the River Mother," they cried as one.

"No!" Tekanu cried. "He's already injured. We mustn't hurt him." Her warriors closed ranks around her. They raised their tridents.

Jarell could hear the desperation in the River Mother's voice as she kept on calling out for her son, but he also knew that it was the warriors' job to protect the River Mother and their home. The Utelif was free. And he was angry.

Kimisi tugged his arm and pointed. "Look."

Jarell spotted it immediately. The gleam of the pearl on the ground. It was a few feet away.

They hurried towards it, but the way was blocked by guards and pulses from their tridents as they tried to protect the River Mother from the raging Utelif.

Kimisi gave a low growl. "We're never going to get to that pearl. Jarell, this griot's song is not for you." She let out a high, keening call and everyone except Jarell covered their ears. Even the Utelif froze in place.

Raising his staff above him, Jarell summoned

the power of the Iron Leopard. He rocketed forward through the water and scooped up the pearl.

Kimisi followed. She swam round to the other side of the Utelif and, as it began to thrash about once more, she let out another high-pitched chant.

The Utelif's movement slowed as Jarell's movement sped up. *I just need to touch him with the pearl. That will break the curse.* The creature's eyes centred on Jarell and then the pendant in his clutches. It gave a low whine, its eyes almost hopeful.

"Yes," Jarell said out loud. "This will help you." He reached out with the pearl and then saw the creature's eyes fill with rage once more. It charged at Jarell, horn down.

The power of the Iron Leopard gave Jarell the speed to get out of its way, but only just. He didn't see the huge scaly tail whip through the water until it was too late. It hit him in the chest, and every scrap of air was forced from his lungs as pain exploded across his body. Water rushed past him as he was catapulted across the cavern.

"Jarell!" screamed Kimisi.

He smashed into the rocky wall of the cavern.

"I'm OK," he muttered, but as he went to

stand, his vision blurred and a wave of dizziness washed over him.

Jarell took a deep breath, but there was nothing to inhale. His lungs were burning, desperate for oxygen. He flicked on the diving suit's display on his arm and a warning flashed up: ERROR. OXYGEN CONNECTOR ERROR.

"Can't . . . breathe," he called weakly over the transmitter.

"Hang on," Kimisi called. "I'm coming!"

He could hear the Utelif's angry calls echoing through the water, but he ignored them. A diagram flashed up on the power cuff, showing where the tear in his oxy-neuro mesh was. Running his hand over his visor, he tried desperately to find the rip. But it was getting harder with every passing second. His fingers, arms and mind were getting heavier and heavier. Darkness crept over him as his fingers trailed across the bed of the lake.

Suddenly, Jarell saw Fades. His cousin's barbershop was full of life – people getting their fresh haircuts – and his paintings hung on the walls.

*But normally the symbol in my hair burns when it's time to return.*

He felt certain that all he needed to do was let go and he would be free.

*Maybe I'm not a true hero after all.*

*But you are a hero, Jarell . . .*

Kundi had returned. His ancestor's voice echoed through Jarell's mind. Some of the darkness retreated.

*You are so close, Jarell. The Iron Crocodile is so very, very near. Remember, water is its home, its power. Draw on that power, Jarell. Find your home in the water.*

Something in his hand vibrated. *The Staff of*

*Kundi*. How had it got there? *The Iron Crocodile is near. Water is its home,* Kundi had said. *Draw on its power.*

Jarell didn't have much time left. There was no air left in his lungs, but the vision of Fades had vanished. He could see Kimisi trying to dodge past the Utelif to get to him. *It was now or never.*

*Time to be a hero . . .*

He deactivated his helmet and it folded back so Jarell could feel cool water on his face. He clasped the staff tightly, and he could feel a power nearby that felt almost prehistoric. He didn't know how, but he breathed in deep through his nose and slithered full-speed through the water, heading straight for the Utelif's horn. At the last moment Jarell swerved, flinging the pendant with all his strength. He watched the pearl and its chain travel through the water and land on the creature's jagged horn.

The Utelif let out a cry far louder than Kimisi's could ever be. Sound waves pulsed through the water. Its tail and head thrashed.

And then the beast started to shrink. Its head became more and more human, and the long sharp horn faded in the dim light.

Jarell sighed in relief and then started to splutter. *Hey, I'm breathing underwater,* he thought. Everything began to feel heavy again. *Correction. I* was *breathing underwater.* His sight blurred and then everything went black.

# CHAPTER TWELVE

## CLOSE CALL

A flash of yellow forced Jarell's eyes wide open. *Titanium-yellow,* he thought. *Just like one of my new pencils.*

Crouching over him was a young merman in a suit of armour made of yellow shells. He looked around the same age as Lucas. The merman smiled and reached under the layers of shells to pull out the Iron Crocodile. The iron head was a deep green, and had a jewelled eye that looked out fiercely.

The Staff of Kundi glowed with a brilliant golden light, and the Iron Crocodile flipped through the water and landed on top of the Iron Leopard. The leopard's eyes shone red as its mouth stretched open and roared a welcome. In response, the Iron Crocodile opened its jaws to reveal a dark-green light deep in its throat. The whole staff thrummed with power, and a cascade of bubbles poured from the crocodile's mouth on to Jarell. They clung to him, covering every inch of his body until they created a second skin of air.

"I can breathe!" Jarell gasped. The suit still flashed a warning about the disconnected oxygen tube, but his lungs were no longer screaming from the lack of air.

*The Iron Crocodile. It's at home underwater. It's helping me breathe!*

Jarell looked around for the merman and spotted him embracing his mother. Jarell felt a sharp spike of homesickness. He really missed his family. He could really do with one of his mum's hugs right now.

"Are you OK?" Kimisi asked, swimming over to him. "You can breathe?"

Jarell nodded.

Kimisi glanced at the staff in his hand. "The Iron Crocodile – you found it!"

"*We* found it," Jarell replied. "Two heads are better than one, remember?"

Just then, Tekanu and her son floated through the water. The warriors stood, watching and smiling.

"You risked your lives for us, even though you weren't sure you could trust me. Thank you," Tekanu said. "I am only sorry I couldn't tell you why I needed your help – from the start."

"If she had, Ikala's curse would have become permanent," her son explained. "I'm Owu, prince of Uchawa. It was my choice to hide the Iron Crocodile from Ikala, and I paid the price of his rage."

Tekanu took her son's hand and gave it a

squeeze. "Imagine creating a curse that can only be broken by someone figuring out the puzzle all by themselves. Ikala has a *wicked* mind."

"We are deeply grateful," the prince said. "Thank you."

"You need to thank the Inkya," Jarell said.

"The Inkya also ask if you would please return the pearl to them," Kimisi added.

Tekanu was silent.

Jarell frowned. "Sonbi told me that you're not *allies* with the Inkya, but things change, right?" He glanced at Kimisi and smiled. "Besides, we all need help from our friends sometimes."

"We will return the pearl," the prince said. "We promise. It will be a new era of peace between us and the Inkya."

"Good. I also—" Before Jarell could finish,

a wave of fiery pain struck the back of his head. He let out a gasp and rubbed where the zigzag symbol was now burning.

"Are you injured?" Tekanu asked in concern. "Do you need the healing pearl? We merpeople specialize in medicines of the sea."

"No, no. It's time for me to return to my world," Jarell said. "The symbol in my hair is what allowed me to come here to Ulfrika, but it also tells me when it is time to go home."

"Ah, now I see the trickster's work in this," the River Mother replied. "Olegu?"

Kimisi sighed. "Yes, indeed. He's part of the team apparently."

"Legsy is a good man," Jarell said. "I'll convince you of that one day, Kimisi." The symbol burned again. "OK, I've got to get back to my world, or I'll be trapped here."

"Descendant of Kundi, it is my turn to help you," Tekanu said. "Although this will not entirely repay my debt to you."

She drifted forward. With a low chant, the River Mother wove a pattern in the water with her hands. An eddy rose from the bottom of the cavern and began to spin. It picked up sand and pebbles and they clashed together, merging and melding until they formed a mirror sheet on the ground. In the surface, Jarell could see the VIP room of Fades, with Legsy pacing around it.

"Eh, it is a strange world you come from," Kimisi said, peering over his shoulder.

Jarell grinned. "Maybe you can come and visit sometime."

Kimisi frowned. "I'll have to think very carefully about that."

"Jarell!" Legsy shouted from the other side, looking up through the mirror at him. "You're cutting it close!"

"Olegu," Tekanu said quietly, although the startled look on Legsy's face showed he'd heard her clearly. "I have not yet had my say on the mess you have created."

Legsy rubbed the back of his neck and let out a nervous laugh. "I am . . . What I mean is . . ." he said. "I will make it up to everyone, Tekanu. I'm *trying* to make it up. I found the Future Hero, didn't I?"

Tekanu's jaw clenched. "Only Olegu would risk someone else's life and call that a solution."

Kimisi and Jarell shared a look. The River Mother had done exactly the same thing when she sent them on their quest to find the pearl.

*These gods and goddesses have very short memories,* Jarell thought.

Kimisi pushed Jarell towards the glass on the ground. Jarell handed the Staff of Kundi to her. "Take good care of it."

"As if my life depends on it," his friend replied. "And we still have two more Iron Animals to find before Ikala, so hurry back, eh?"

Jarell stepped on to the glass. Tekanu and Owu waved goodbye.

"See you soon, heir of Kundi," Kimisi said.

"See you soon," Jarell said, and then he was falling through the abyss and landing back on the barbershop floor, almost in a handstand.

He rolled it into a cartwheel, narrowly missing Legsy's broom and bin, and found himself back on his feet.

"Show-off," Legsy said, but he was smiling. "It

is good to have you back."

"It's good to be back!" Jarell said.

"Come on, you'd better sit down in the chair and let me fix your hair," Legsy said.

Jarell rubbed the back of his head. There was a smooth patch of skin where the symbol had been.

Legsy took out his clippers and began to give Jarell a low fade. "I'm telling you, if you'd got home sooner, then we wouldn't have to do this."

Jarell raised an eyebrow at Legsy in the mirror. "There was a lot to do."

"Indeed, I saw some of it. I told you those Manatees were a sign."

"Yep, you were definitely right about tha—" Jarell stopped as soon as he heard the rattle of the beaded curtain. They both turned.

"Jarell! Legsy!" Omari said. "How long does a cut take?"

"I am an artist, young Omari," Legsy said with a sniff.

Omari chuckled. "My bad. Listen, Jarell, Lucas just called. He said you weren't picking up your phone."

"What's wrong?" Jarell asked.

"Apparently your mum wants you both to go swimming," Omari said. "The leisure centre is doing some kind of free course with the lifeguard."

Jarell's shoulders slumped. *I really have had enough of the water and life-saving.* He bet Lucas didn't want to go either, although Lucas loved beating him in swimming races.

Jarell sat up straighter in the chair. *But maybe not this time.* Jarell smiled at the thought. *I've had a lot of practice, after all.*

# LEGEND OF THE FUTURE HERO

Kundi was the finest hero to ever live in the land of Ulfrika. He was famed for his powers of healing, he loved to study the wildlife and found a rich gold mine in the Muho Desert and shared his wealth.

Ikala was an evil sorcerer who wanted to rule all of Ulfrika with an iron fist. Kundi defeated Ikala years ago, but Ikala and his army was so powerful, Kundi had to gather allies from every corner of Ulfrika to have a chance of winning. And even then, he was only able to imprison Ikala.

Over the years, Kundi's descendants travelled the realms, including to our world, leaving the Staff of Kundi, a powerful weapon, in the safe hands of the Goddess Ayana.

After centuries of plotting and planning, Ikala managed to break free using trickery. He came to the temple of Ayana to get the Staff of Kundi, the only weapon that could defeat him. But the Goddess Ayana split the staff into pieces, spreading its four Iron Animal heads – leopard, eagle, crocodile, snake – across the country using storm magic.

Now Ulfrika waits for the prophesized Future Hero, the Heir of Kundi, to return to their realm as he is the only person who can defeat Ikala with the Staff of Kundi. But first he must find the Iron Animals before Ikala does and reassemble the Staff. Otherwise, Ikala will take over Ulfrika and then begin to seek out new worlds to rule, including ours. . .

Once Jarell was identified as the Future Hero, he travelled to Ulfrika and found the Iron Leopard at Fire Mountain with the help of his warrior-friend Kimisi.

# TEKANU
## THE RIVER MOTHER OF THE MERPEOPLE

**POWERS:** Control of the currents and flow of water, can create portals back to our world/Earth

**SKILLS:** Sings a powerful and calming song

**AGE:** Ancient

**ABOUT:** She has long locs which flow like a river down her back; has seaweed decorating her hair and wears a tall, regal coral crown. She has rainbow-coloured scales down the sides of her face and neck and wears flowing blue robes. She is neither an ally of Kundi or Ikala; her loyalty is to her own people.

# PEOPLE OF ULFRIKA

# MERPEOPLE

- The River Mother's subjects are merpeople and she has different kinds of warriors that protect her
- The merpeople have gold and turquoise eyes, fins that sprout from their arms and legs and gills instead of ears
- Their city grows out of the lakebed like a giant tree, and is covered in pulsing electrical blue circuits. It is taller than the buildings in London
- Merpeople specialize in medicines of the sea

# INKYA

*There are many, many stories about them. It is said that if a traveller does anything to disrespect the sea, the Inkya take them to the Shadow Sea Forest – never to be seen again.*

- The Inkya are the legendary Sea Horse people of the Shadow Sea Forest
- They are said to be secretive, strong and powerful
- Their bodies are covered in fine stripes; they have fins, long horse-like muzzles and powerful serpent-like tails
- The Inkya soldiers wear armour and gold

# CREATURES OF ULFRIKA

# UTELIF

***Find the cure before the Utelif destroys … or is destroyed.***

- The Utelif is a great whale with yellow and green scales and a large, jagged horn
- Utelifs like to live in saltwater such as the Shadow Sea
- In this story, the Utelif has been cursed by Ikala and the only cure is the pearl pendant

# MANATEES

- Manatees have thick, round bodies like a hippo, and short flipper-like arms
- Bool and Chip are two Manatees that help Jarell and Kimisi to find the Shadow Sea
- They speak in rhyme and their language sounds like whistles, but Kimisi's translator helps the heroes understand them
- They are from the Koffi River and have a pleasant nature with bright and happy smiles

# THE ZIN

- The Zin is made from thousands of tiny creatures and it appears as an eerie mist of colourful light
- Ikala brought the tiny creatures together to attack the Inkya people – one touch from the Zin can turn you to stone
- Jarell comes up with a plan to defeat the Zin with the help of the Inkya

# PLACES IN ULFRIKA

# THE SHADOW SEA FOREST & THE INKYA CITY

The Inkya city lies beyond the Shadow Sea Forest, which is made of huge, thick seaweed, taller than mountains.

In the Shadow Sea Forest, there is a tall building made of twisted red and orange coral with holes for doors and windows. Inside, the building is decorated with swirls of multi-coloured sand. This is where Jarell and Kimisi first find Sonbi – a leader of the Inkya – who has been turned to stone by the Zin.

The city of the Inkya is made up of coral buildings. At the centre of the city is the palace, covered in sparkling sea glass and near that is The Tower of Breath – a fountain of bubbles made of coral, some bleached with age. The Tower of Breath holds a secret chamber covered in golden seaweed where the pearl pendant, with the power to cure all illnesses, was hidden.

# MAGICAL OBJECTS

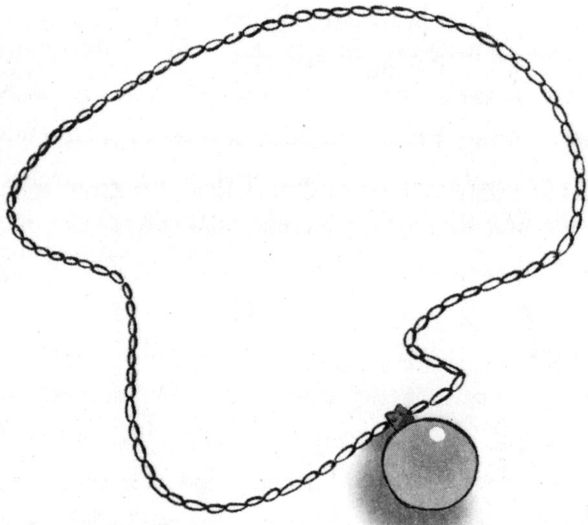

# PEARL PENDANT

- This is a golden chain with a large pearl hanging from it
- It can heal any illness and lift curses with a single touch
- Kundi once borrowed the pearl pendant from the Inkya to save a sea creature called the Walé

# STAFF OF KUNDI

- It was created to stop the evil sorcerer Ikala
- Only an heir of Kundi can use its full power
- There are four sculpted Iron Animals stacked at the top of the staff – a leopard, an eagle, a crocodile and a snake
- Each animal has a unique power and can control a different element
- To keep it out of the hands of Ikala, the goddess Ayana split the staff up into the separate Iron Animals
- As Jarell journeys across Ulfrika to find the missing Iron Animals, the staff reassembles in a new order
- The Iron Leopard has the power of fire and speed, and was retrieved from a Volcano in Ekpani
- The Iron Crocodile has the power of water and was retrieved from the Shadow Sea Forest